if you're

clueless

about

buying a

home

and
want to
know more

if you're

clueless

about

buying a home

and

want to

know more

DAVID W. MYERS

DEARBORN™
A **Kaplan Professional** Company

If You're Clueless about Buying a Home and Want to Know More

Series Creator: Seth Godin
Acquisitions Editor: Jean Iversen
Managing Editor: Jack Kiburz
Interior and Cover Design: Karen Engelmann
Typesetting: Omega Publishing Services, Inc.

© 1999 by Lark Productions

Published by Dearborn, a Kaplan Professional Company

Printed in the United States of America

99 00 01 10 9 8 7 6 5 4 3 2

Library of Congress Cataloging-in-Publication Data

Myers, David W.
    If you're clueless about buying a home and want to know more /
David W. Myers.
        p.   cm.
    Includes index.
    ISBN 0-7931-3112-X (paper)
    1. House buying—United States. 2. Residential real estate-
-United States—Purchasing. 3. Real estate business—United States.
I. Title.
HD255.M927 1999
643'.12'0973—dc21   99-12038
                                                             CIP

Dearborn books are available at special quantity discounts to use as premiums and sales promotions, or for use in corporate training programs. For more information, please call the Special Sales Manager at 800-621-9621, ext. 4514, or write to Dearborn Financial Publishing, Inc., 155 North Wacker Drive, Chicago, IL 60606-1719.

This book is dedicated to Carole, Drake, and "Baby Miranda"—
and to my parents, Ray and Dorothy, whose love and encouragement
to their six children made our humble house the best home of all.

Other Clueless Books

Acknowledgments

Poet John Donne wrote that "no man is an island, entire of itself." He could've added that no writer is a book author unto himself, for it takes a lot of talented people to put a book like this together.

First and foremost, I'd like to thank Karen Watts for editing this tome and for the invaluable advice and support she provided as the manuscript was pulled together. Karen is the driving force behind the fast-growing Clueless series, and her insight into what makes a "how-to" book successful provided this longtime newspaper reporter with the guidance needed to write his first book.

Some other props are in order here. Many thanks to the National Association of REALTORS®, especially Jeff Lubar, Trisha Riggs, and Liz Johnson of NAR's Public Affairs Department, for providing access to the trade association's vast array of resources. Thanks also to Bradley Inman of the Emeryville, California-based Inman News Features (http://www.inman.com), who pioneered the concept of bringing helpful real estate information to consumers over the Internet in 1995.

My heartfelt thanks also go to Willemijn de Clercq, Bryan Mistele, and the rest of the talented "real estate revolutionaries" at Microsoft Corporation. The time I spent helping to create their HomeAdvisor.com Web site in 1998 was well worth all those rainy days I weathered at Microsoft's headquarters in Redmond, Washington.

There are two more people that I'd like to thank. The first is Maria Carmacino, the longtime editor of my nationally syndicated "About Real Estate" column, who recently left King Features Syndicate after 22 years of dedicated service. The second is Dick Turpin, the legendary real estate editor of *The Los Angeles Times,* who earned a Pulitzer Prize in the course of covering L.A.'s emergence as a "nice little post-war" town in the 1940s to its position as the nation's second-largest city and undisputed Capital of the Pacific Rim today. I was privileged to work under the tutelage of "Ol' Turp," who retired in 1989 but still knows more about the real estate business than any other journalist I've met in the three decades that I have spent helping people to buy and sell homes.

Contents

GETTING a clue about Buying A HOME

Buying a home is an exciting and fun process, but it's not just a chance to live out your domestic fantasies. There's a lot involved: time, responsibility, money— the works. Make sure you know what you're getting into and that you're ready to take that step.

Buying a home can be one of the most exciting, fulfilling, and profitable experiences that you'll ever enjoy. It's your chance to stake out a little corner of the earth to call your own, to put down roots, and to start building some equity instead of wasting your money on rent. As a bonus, your home will probably rise steadily in value and Uncle Sam will give you lots of tax breaks to subsidize your monthly payments.

Still, not everyone's cut out to be a homeowner. Some people can't buy a house because they can't seem to scrape together enough cash to make even the smallest down payment or they don't earn enough to persuade a bank to give them a loan. Other people simply shouldn't buy a home—at least not today—because they won't live in the property long enough to recoup all their money when they sell or they're just not ready to make such a major commitment of their time and money.

Commitment. In the end, that's really all it takes to buy a home. As you'll see in chapter 2, you don't need a truckload of cash to purchase your first house, co-op, or condominium. There are plenty of people who can help in your homebuying quest (chapter 3) and in narrowing down your search to the two or three most promising properties (chapter 4).

Chapter 5 will show you how to avoid paying too much for the home you want to buy and includes sample wording of two simple but powerful paragraphs to include in your offer that can let you get all your money back if the deal turns sour. Chapter 6 provides tried-and-true strategies to successfully (and quickly) wrap-up negotiations with the seller and settle disputes that might arise if your all-important home inspection uncovers major problems.

It's a statistical fact that the traditional 30-year mortgage lasts twice as long as a typical marriage. This book won't help you find the best mate or solve your marital problems, but chapter 7 will help you choose the perfect mortgage to finance your purchase and live happily with your loan for years to come.

Chapter 8 demystifies the closing process and tells you how to solve the most common problems that can arise between the time your offer is accepted and the day you get the keys to your new home. Chapter 9 provides money-saving tips to cut your housing-related costs after you move in, practical strategies for dealing with nettlesome neighborhood issues, and an easy-to-use worksheet to determine when refinancing your original loan makes good financial sense.

A Word about the Internet

By some accounts, there are now more than 50,000 real estate related Web sites available for free on the Internet—that vast network of telephone lines, high-tech gizmos, and electronic information that's doubling in size every few months. Even if you were willing to spend 40 hours a week visiting each of today's housing-related Web pages for just five minutes each, you'd spend the next two years of your life in front of a computer searching for the handful of sites that provide useful information rather than marketing pitches for sales agents, lenders, and operators of get-rich-quick scams.

Don't worry: We've typed our chubby fingers to the bone, searching out the best sites for you. Sprinkled throughout this book are the Web addresses of many of the most useful Internet sites for homebuyers. In this book you'll find everything you need to know about buying a house and getting the best deal, but visiting the Web sites we mention can supplement the information we provide and give you access to handy online calculators and other resources that can only be found on the Internet.

If you don't have a computer with Internet access, one of your friends probably does. Many libraries and universities also offer free or low-cost Internet access to the general public.

Buying versus Renting

From a financial perspective, almost everyone would be better off owning a home instead of renting. You might think that's hogwash, especially if you compare the "for rent" ads in your local newspaper with the "for sale" ads and find that, say, the $750 you're currently paying to rent is a lot less than the $1,000-a-month mortgage payments it would take to purchase a comparable home.

Sure, the monthly payments involved in owning are almost always higher than the cost of renting. But homeowners are allowed to claim a variety of special tax breaks that, in many cases, actually makes the cost of owning a home lower than the cost of renting.

Big Tax Breaks

Say you're looking at a house, and the owner will either sell it to you—in which case your mortgage payments would be $1,000 a month—or will lease it to you for $750 a month. In one year you'd make $12,000 in mortgage payments if you purchased the house, or $9,000 in rental payments if you leased it. Renting instead of buying would save you $3,000 a year, right?

Wrong. By buying the house, you'd get to deduct all of your mortgage interest payments. Because almost all of the payments in the first few years of a loan go toward interest, you'd automatically be entitled to nearly $12,000 in deductions (plus even

more write-offs for your property taxes and the like). If you're in the typical 28 percent federal tax bracket, $12,000 in deductions would save you $3,360 in taxes ($12,000 x .28 = $3,360). In short, the *after-tax* cost of owning the home in the first year would be $8,640—or $360 less than renting it.

Owning instead of renting would save you even more if you live in a state that levies its own income taxes because you'd get to claim the deductions on both your state and federal returns.

VISIT THE WEB

The Internet Web site operated by The Homebuyer's Fair features a nifty online calculator to help you determine whether it makes sense for you to buy a home now or continue to rent, based on your potential tax savings and other factors. Go to http://www.homefair.com and click the "first-time buyer" line under the "Guides" heading.

Appreciating Appreciation

Of course, there's another financial benefit of owning rather than renting: You, not a landlord, will get to keep any increase in the value of the property.

Before we go on, let's face facts: There's no guarantee that the value of your property will rise, not fall. Home prices tend to move with changes in the local and national economy, which means the value of the home you buy could decline if key employers in the area start to layoff workers or the U.S. plunges into recession. You shouldn't delay your homebuying plans because you're worried about what might happen several years from now. But you'd be foolish to buy today if it's apparent that your community is in for rough times in the near future or your own job is in jeopardy.

Though price gains aren't guaranteed, they almost always occur. The value of a typical U.S. home has increased an average of 5 percent annually over the past 30 years. That trend should continue as the population grows, as land prices and construction expenses increase, and as inflation pushes the cost of virtually everything else higher. Odds are, if you buy now, your home will likely be worth much more when you eventually decide to sell.

Buying a house will also protect you from future rent increases. Like home values, apartment rents have also been rising an average of 5 percent a year. If home values and rents both keep going up at a 5 percent clip, here's what you can expect to pay to buy a home or rent an apartment in the future:

Cost today	In 3 years	In 5 years	In 10 years	In 20 years	In 30 years
$125,000 home	$144,703	$159,535	$203,612	$331,662	$540,243
$700 rental	$810	$893	$1,140	$1,857	$3,025

This chart really tells you two things. First, buying a home might seem like an expensive proposition today but it's not going to be any cheaper a few years from now. And second, if you buy now you stand a pretty good chance of making a lot of money when you sell later.

Who Should Rent?

Even though owning a house can provide important financial and psychological rewards, some people are still better off renting instead of buying. Seriously consider continuing to rent if you fall into one of the following categories:

- *You plan to move again within two years.* Buyers typically spend an amount equal to about 5 percent of their purchase price on loan fees and other transaction-related costs. Sellers usually pay an amount equal to 10 percent, including a 6 percent sales commission and other fees. If you sold the home a year after moving in, the value of your property would have to increase a staggering 15 percent—three times the historic average—just for you to break even. Even if you waited two years, the property would have to climb an above-average 7.5 percent a year for you to get all your money back. Unless home values in your area are skyrocketing, you're better off renting if you don't expect to live in your new home for at least three years.

- *You don't have much spare time.* Owning a home and keeping it in good shape takes time. Unless you've got enough cash to hire a gardener and professional repairpeople, you can expect to spend countless hours mowing, painting, making repairs, and performing dozens of other chores.

Renters usually don't have to worry about such mundane matters; they can simply call their landlord.

- *You're in an area where home prices are falling.* It's tempting to buy a house the moment that prices decline, hoping to pick up a bargain. Truth is, what you'll likely be doing is the equivalent of buying a ticket on the Titanic because price declines tend to snowball. Keep renting until you're sure home values have stabilized. Then you can capitalize on the bargain-basement prices and greatly increase your chance of making a handsome profit when you sell.

- *Your job or personal finances are on shaky ground.* You certainly don't want to buy a house if you're seriously concerned that you're about to lose your job, especially if finding a new job with comparable pay will be difficult. Nor should you buy a house if you're overwhelmed with debt and can barely make ends meet. Keep renting until your employment status stabilizes and your finances are under control. Besides, no reputable lender will give you a mortgage if you can't prove that you've got the financial wherewithal to pay the money back.

Take the two-minute exam on pages 7–8 to get a better idea of whether you're really ready to become a homeowner.

How Much Home Can You Afford?

Real estate agents, lenders, and even some book authors like to offer handy little rules of thumb to give prospective buyers an idea of how much they can pay for a house. One says you should figure on spending an amount that's equal to two-and-a-half times your annual income. Another says the magic figure is roughly equal to 200 times the monthly rent you might be paying now. Yet another old rule says you should multiply one-fourth your annual income by 15 or 20 to figure out how much you can afford to pay.

Like old shoes, these old rules belong in the garbage. They may have worked 20 years ago, when lenders made only fixed-rate loans and the only choice a buyer had was to pick either a 30-year or 15-year repayment schedule. But as you'll see in chapter 7,

Are You Really Ready to Buy a Home?

Buying a home involves a major commitment of both time and money. Answer the 10 true-false questions below to determine if you're really ready to buy a home. Some of your answers are more important than others. When you're done, add up your points and see the results below.

1. If I buy a home, I don't plan on moving again for at least two years. (Worth eight points)

   ___ True   ___ False

2. My job is secure and there's little chance I will lose it. (Eight points)

   ___ True   ___ False

3. I've done some preliminary checking, and home prices in my area appear to be increasing. (Eight points)

   ___ True   ___ False

4. I have at least $5,000 or $10,000 available to use for a down payment and pay my sales-related closing costs. (Seven points)

   ___ True   ___ False

5. I'm willing to spend at least 40 hours looking for the best home that I can afford. (Four points)

   ___ True   ___ False

6. I'm willing to cut back on my other expenses if it's the only way I can afford to buy a home. (Four points)

   ___ True   ___ False

7. I pay my bills on time, and haven't made more than two late payments in the last two years. (Four points)

    ___ True   ___ False

8. My housing needs won't change much over the next two years. (Three points)

    ___ True   ___ False

9. I don't expect my first home to be my "dream house." (Two points)

    ___ True   ___ False

10. I'm willing to devote at least a couple of hours a week to keep my home looking nice and in good repair. (Two points)

    ___ True   ___ False

What Your Score Means

All questions answered "True" are worth the designated number of points. All "False" answers are worth zero points. Add 'em up and check out your score.

Score

43–50: You're a great candidate to buy a house now.

35–42: Your prospects are good, but double-check your finances and priorities.

28–34: You can still buy a house, but it's going to take hard work and sacrifice.

 0–27: Delay your homebuying plans until you can handle such a major commitment.

today's buyers can choose from dozens of different financing plans. The lender and mortgage program you select will have a huge impact on how much you can borrow, which in turn will determine how much you can pay for a home.

The other problem with those old rules of thumb is that they automatically assume that everyone's financial situation is the same. All men are created equal, but all borrowers are not. If you earn $50,000 a year, have plenty of cash for a down payment, and boast a sterling credit record, you might easily be able to buy a home whose price tag is four, five, or even six times your annual salary. But no conventional lender will let you borrow a nickel if you haven't been able to save at least a fraction of your $50,000 income for a down payment, if your credit cards are over their limits, and if the repo man just hauled away your car.

There are really only two ways to get a good estimate of how much you can borrow and, thus, figure out how much house you can afford. You can visit a mortgage broker or lender for help or you can do the calculations yourself. If you use a real estate agent to help in your house-hunting efforts, the agent may also be able to give you a good idea of how much you can borrow.

What Lenders Look For

Lenders consider a variety of factors to determine how much you're eligible to borrow, which in turn determines how much you can afford to pay for a home. The only concept you have to grasp right now involves what bankers call your *debt ratios*.

Most lenders use two ratios when evaluating your loan application. The first, your *front-end ratio,* reflects how much of your gross (pretax) monthly income would be needed to pay your housing expenses. The second, the *back-end ratio,* measures how much of your pay would be gobbled up by your housing expenses and minimum payments on your credit card balances and other debts.

Generally, most lenders use a front-end ratio of 28 percent and a back-end ratio of 36 percent. In other words, no more than 28 percent of your pretax monthly pay could be used to pay the four components of your mortgage—principal, interest, taxes, and insurance (PITI). Payments on your home and all your other bills couldn't eat up more than 36 percent of your pay.

VISIT THE WEB

You can get a good idea of how much you can borrow based on your current financial situation by using the "affordability calculator" on the Web site operated by online giant Quicken (http://www.quicken.com). Click the "affordability" line under the "Home and Mortgage" heading.

The higher your ratios, the less you can borrow. Say you earn $45,000 a year, which works out to $3,750 per month. Your monthly mortgage payments, including a reserve for property taxes and hazard insurance, would not be allowed to exceed $1,050 (28 percent). Your mortgage payments and monthly payments on all your other debt couldn't exceed $1,350 (36 percent) of your gross pay.

The table on page 11 will give you a better idea of how ratios can determine your borrowing power, assuming that you have an average credit rating and want to apply for a 30-year, fixed-rate mortgage. To use it, find your gross annual income in the first column. The second column represents what your monthly payment would be, assuming that 25 percent of your income will be used to pay for principal and interest and another 3 percent will be earmarked for property taxes and insurance. The top line is the interest rate you'd be charged.

To use the chart and get a ballpark idea of how much you can borrow, simply find the point where your gross income and the interest rate intersect.

The Last Word on Ratios

Although all lenders use ratios, some have more generous standards than others. While the 28/36 figures are the industry's benchmarks, some lenders will let you devote up to 35 percent of your income to make your mortgage payments and up to 45 percent for housing expenses and all your other bills. Many buyers seek out these high-ratio lenders so they can get a bigger loan to buy a more expensive house. Other buyers use them because they don't earn enough to meet the common 28/36 guidelines. But because high-ratio loans are considered riskier—after all, it means that your housing bills and other debts will be taking an extra-large bite out of your paycheck—lenders who make the loans typically charge higher rates and sometimes demand a minimum down payment of at least 20 percent.

Estimating Your Borrowing Power

Gross Annual Income	Monthly Payment	6.5%	7%	7.5%	8.0%	8.5%	9.0%	9.5%	10%	10.5%
$ 20,000	$ 417	65,921	62,628	59,591	56,785	54,189	51,784	49,553	47,480	45,550
25,000	521	82,401	78,285	74,488	70,981	67,736	64,730	61,941	59,349	56,938
30,000	625	98,882	93,942	89,386	85,177	81,284	77,676	74,329	71,219	68,325
35,000	729	115,362	109,599	104,284	99,373	94,831	90,622	86,717	83,089	79,713
40,000	833	131,842	125,256	119,181	113,570	108,378	103,568	99,106	94,959	91,101
45,000	938	148,323	140,913	134,079	127,766	121,925	116,514	111,494	106,829	102,488
50,000	1,042	164,803	156,570	148,977	141,962	135,473	129,460	123,882	118,699	113,876
55,000	1,146	181,283	172,227	163,874	156,158	149,020	142,406	136,270	130,569	125,263
60,000	1,250	197,764	187,884	178,772	170,354	162,567	155,352	148,658	142,439	136,651
65,000	1,354	214,244	203,541	193,670	184,551	176,114	168,298	161,047	154,308	148,039
70,000	1,458	230,724	219,199	208,567	198,747	189,662	181,244	173,435	166,178	159,426
75,000	1,563	247,204	234,856	223,465	212,943	203,209	194,190	185,823	178,048	170,814
80,000	1,667	263,685	250,513	238,363	227,139	216,756	207,136	198,211	189,918	182,201
85,000	1,771	280,165	266,170	253,260	241,335	230,303	220,082	210,599	201,788	193,589
90,000	1,875	296,645	281,827	268,158	255,532	243,851	233,028	222,988	213,658	204,976
95,000	1,979	313,126	297,484	283,056	269,728	257,398	245,975	235,376	225,528	216,364
100,000	2,083	329,606	313,141	297,953	283,924	270,945	258,921	247,764	237,398	227,752
110,000	2,292	362,566	344,455	327,749	312,316	298,040	284,813	272,540	261,137	250,527
120,000	2,500	395,527	375,769	357,544	340,709	325,134	310,705	297,317	284,877	273,302

As an alternative to using a high-ratio lender, try to pay off some of your current debt before applying for a mortgage and save more money so you can make a bigger down payment. Meeting the lending industry's preset 28/36 standards will help to ensure that you get the lowest possible interest rate while also protecting you from drowning in debt.

Prequalifying versus Preapproval

In real estate jargon, the process involved in using ratios to get an estimate of how much you can borrow is called *prequalifying*. It's an important step to take before you start shopping for a home, largely because it will help you avoid wasting time looking at properties that you simply cannot afford.

Say you've scraped together $20,000 to make a down payment and cover your sales-related closing costs. If you've prequalified yourself (or had a lender do it for you) and found that you could borrow about $120,000, you could save a lot of time by limiting your house-hunting search to properties offered in the range of $120,000 to $150,000. Properties offered for as much as $170,000 might even be within your reach because, as you'll see in chapter 5, it's often very easy to get sellers to settle for less than their asking price. But looking at homes priced at more than $180,000 or so would likely be a waste of your time. Even if you could persuade the seller to provide a hefty $20,000 discount, your high debt ratios would probably prevent you from getting a loan that's big enough to finance the transaction.

Why Preapproval Is Better

Though getting prequalified is a good move, getting preapproved for a mortgage is even better.

While it's possible to prequalify yourself to get a ballpark idea of how much you can borrow, getting preapproved takes a little more time and almost always involves actually sitting down with a lender or mortgage broker. You'll show the lender lots of documentation—recent pay stubs, tax returns, copies of your credit card statements, and the like—and the lender will then issue you a letter or card that indicates how much you can borrow based on your current financial situation, credit rating, and other factors.

Getting a lender's preapproval letter is much better than getting prequalified. It encourages you to begin gathering up all the documents you'll need to get a loan now, reducing the chance that you'll encounter costly last-minute delays later. More importantly, it gives you a big advantage over buyers who haven't been preapproved and more negotiating power with the seller. After all, if you were a seller whose offer would you accept: A bid from a buyer who has already proven her creditworthiness to a bank and has been preapproved for a mortgage or an offer from a buyer who hasn't even visited a lender and has no idea how much he can borrow?

Most lenders will be happy to prequalify you for free. But many charge a fee of $200 or more to issue a formal preapproval because it involves so much extra work. If you're required to pay a fee, ask the lender if the money can be credited to your account when your loan closes. Some lenders routinely issue such refunds, but only if the borrower is savvy enough to request one. You can't get the money back if you don't ask for it.

And if you want to enjoy a purely electronic experience, visit www.quicken.com and work up your prequalification online.

Of Bankers and Brokers, Income and Debts

Unless your last name is Rockefeller or you've just hit the lottery, you're going to need a lender to help finance the purchase of your home. There are lots of lenders out there who are willing to help, but you'll have to decide if you want to deal with them yourself or have a mortgage broker act as your intermediary. Both choices have their advantages and drawbacks.

Finding the lender that offers the best mortgage deal yourself takes time. You need to contact at least half a dozen to find the one or two that offer the best financing packages, and you can't rely solely on the ones that advertise heavily because they often charge higher rates or fees to recoup the cost of their marketing campaigns. You'll find tips for finding a good lender and negotiating the best deal in chapter 7.

On its face, enlisting a mortgage broker to find a loan for you seems like a much better idea. Mortgage brokers are authorized to make loans on behalf of several lending institutions instead of only one. You typically don't have to pay for their services because they collect a fee from the lender for bringing in your business and processing most of the loan paperwork.

A good mortgage broker will save you both time and money by doing the loan hunting for you and helping you find the best available rate and terms. A bad broker, on the other hand, won't care about getting the best loan and instead will steer you toward the lender who'll pay that broker the highest fee. Considering this danger, the best way to hunt for a mortgage is to ask your friends or a real estate agent to recommend a mortgage broker who has helped them before. While the broker starts looking for a loan on your behalf, supplement his or her efforts by visiting at least three or four lenders on your own. The broker's work, coupled with your own sleuthing, should help you find the best rates and terms available.

Top Five Things to Do Right Now

1. Take two minutes to complete the "Are You Really Ready to Buy a Home?" exam.

2. Contact a couple of lenders or a mortgage broker to get prequalified for a loan now so you won't waste time looking at properties that you can't afford to buy. Or, prequalify yourself by using the "Estimating Your Borrowing Power" table or by spending a few minutes with the online calculator at http://www.quicken.com.

3. Check newspaper ads or call a few local real estate agents to get a ballpark idea of how much homes in your general area are selling for and whether prices over the past several months have been rising or falling.

4. Remember that the generous tax breaks provided to homeowners often makes buying a home more affordable than renting. Have a real estate agent run the numbers for you or use the online "rent-versus-buy" calculator at http://www.homefair.com.

5. Read the next chapter, "Getting Ready to Buy," to decide which type of home is best for you and to learn how to clean up your credit record to get the best mortgage deal.

Getting READY to BUY?

CHAPTER TWO

Before plunging into the homebuying waters, prioritize your expectations and polish your credit record. These efforts will prevent you from paying too much for a home, allow you to borrow more money, and help you get the best mortgage deal.

Congratulations! Hopefully, the fact that you're starting to read this chapter means you've taken the two-minute test on pages 7–8 and determined that you're ready to become a homeowner. It'll soon be time to start visiting open houses, perusing newspaper ads, and maybe even cruising the Internet to find your first home.

Before you begin your house hunting journey, though, you have to prepare for your trip. The two key essentials you'll need to take along are a clean credit record—or at least a record that puts your credit history in the best possible light—and an understanding that your first home probably won't be your dream house.

In some ways, the main purpose of this chapter is to make sure you've got a firm grip on your homebuying potential. You might be clueless about how the real estate mar-

ket works, but you're certainly no dummy or idiot—you're smart enough to know that a reputable lender won't give you a mortgage unless you have a half-decent credit history. Even the tiniest of errors you can correct on your credit report now will increase the amount of money you can borrow and perhaps even entitle you to a below-market interest rate when you eventually find a home and apply for a loan to close the deal.

Getting a Reality Check

When you were a kid, did you ever jump feetfirst into an inviting pool or lake only to find that the water was cold enough to freeze a penguin? Well, too many first-time buyers jump headfirst into the housing market and have a similarly chilling experience: They're shocked when they find out how little their hard-earned money can buy. Even the most modest home may seem way overpriced, and you might even be so disheartened that you consider scrapping your homebuying plans altogether.

Don't make that mistake. You can't expect your first home to be your dream house, just like a teenager can't expect his or her first car to be a Porsche or Rolls Royce. Home prices might seem high today but they'll probably be even higher tomorrow, next year, or a few years from now. Buying a home now, even if it's smaller than you'd like, will let you take advantage of those rising prices and allow you to begin building some equity so you can eventually sell and use your profits to purchase a nicer property. Continuing to rent would mean continuing to throw your money out the window. Renters don't make themselves rich; they only make landlords rich.

Your Needs versus Your Wants

Although buying a home now will almost certainly require that you make some compromises, it does not mean you'll have to settle for a broken-down rattrap in the worst part of town. The trick to finding the best house you can afford is to make a wish list that's separated into three categories.

1. *Features that you absolutely must have.* Can you get by with only one bathroom or must you have two or three because you've got a large family? Similarly, an extra bedroom or den might be a "must-have" if you work

from home and need a place for your computer and file cabinets. Otherwise, it's a nicety that you probably can live without.

2. *Features you'd like to have, but don't necessarily need.* A spare bedroom or den probably fits into this category unless it's elevated to "must-have" status because you work from home or because there's no way to keep your sanity if you don't have a room where you can watch TV or pursue your hobbies without interruptions from other members of your family. Ditto for a finished basement or attic. An oversized kitchen or extra pantry space also belongs here, unless you're a master chef whose life revolves around cooking or you're a parent who must feed an army of kids every night.

3. *Features you can definitely live without.* Sure, it'd be swell if your first home had a pool, hot tub, private bowling lane, and an oversized yard that's big enough to start a winery. But you can probably forgo such amenities, especially if your homebuying budget is tight and you'd have to give up something from your "must-have" list to keep your purchase price within reason. Also remember that many amenities, including pools and large yards, require lots of maintenance duties that you'd have to perform yourself or pay someone to do for you.

Use the "wants versus needs" checklist on pages 20–21 to determine your minimum housing requirements. Take the completed list with you as you begin looking for a home to buy. It'll help to ensure that any home you purchase will meet your basic needs and also help you to avoid spending a lot of money for "extras" that aren't really important.

Choices, Choices, and More Choices

The checklist we just mentioned is primarily designed to help you decide how large a house you need. But as you begin your house hunting trek, you'll also need to decide what type of home is best for you. Do you want a brand-new home or an older one that may have more charm? Do you want a freestanding house or would you like to save money by purchasing a condominium or other type of attached home? The list

Your "Wants versus Needs" Checklist

Buying your first home will likely require some compromises to keep your purchase price affordable. Review the checklist below and determine how important each feature is to you.

Make a copy of the list and bring it along as you begin visiting open houses. Focusing on the homes that feature everything you really need will help to ensure that you'll be happy with the property you eventually buy and that you won't overpay for "extras" that aren't important.

General Requirements

___ New house   ___ Resale home
___ Doesn't matter

___ Freestanding house   ___ Condo/townhouse/co-op
___ Doesn't matter

___ One story   ___ Two stories
___ Doesn't matter

Minimum number of bedrooms: ___ 1   ___ 2   ___ 3
       ___ 4 or more

Minimum number of bathrooms: ___ 1   ___ 1 1/2   ___ 2
       ___ 2 1/2   ___ 3   ___ 3 1/2
       ___ 4 or more

Specific Requirements

Feature	Must Have	Like to Have	Don't Care
Living room	___	___	___

Feature	Must Have	Like to Have	Don't Care
Dining room	_____	_____	_____
Family room	_____	_____	_____
Den/office	_____	_____	_____
Oversized kitchen	_____	_____	_____
Basement or attic	_____	_____	_____
Finished basement or attic	_____	_____	_____
Garage	_____	_____	_____
Carport	_____	_____	_____
Air conditioning	_____	_____	_____
Fireplace	_____	_____	_____
Large yard	_____	_____	_____
Pool	_____	_____	_____
Hot tub	_____	_____	_____
Short commute to work	_____	_____	_____
Close to public transit	_____	_____	_____
Close to relatives/friends	_____	_____	_____

Other features you must have:

_____

_____

goes on and on. Each choice you're offered is filled with plenty of advantages and drawbacks. Let's take a closer look at the key decisions you will have to make.

Old Home or New?

The most important benefit of buying a brand-new home is that, well, everything is new. There are no worn spots on the carpet, everything is sparkling clean, and you probably won't have to worry about moving in and finding that the roof, plumbing, or electrical system needs an expensive overhaul. Many new homes also offer the latest in design and are loaded with lots of built-in appliances and other amenities.

On the downside, some new homes look like they rolled off an assembly line: Each one appears remarkably like the one next door or across the street. New homes also usually lack the top-notch craftsmanship, quality construction, and character offered by older houses. This is especially true at many new-home tracts designed for first-time buyers because builders must often cut corners to keep their prices affordable and still make a profit.

Older homes are often better-built than new ones. Many feature nice little touches, like curved walls, side molding, and big porches that are too expensive to be included in new houses today. But their age can also present problems. For example, damage wrought by termites or other pests over the years can't easily be seen but is extremely expensive to correct once you buy the home and move in. Many older homes also have outdated wiring systems or worn-out plumbing that can cost a bundle to update or repair. You'll learn how to detect these and other potentially costly problems in chapter 4.

The "Urbs" or the "Burbs"?

You'll also need to decide whether you want to live in or near the downtown urban area or whether you'd feel more comfortable living in an outlying suburb.

Not long ago, the vast majority of homebuyers wanted to live in the suburbs. Their decision was easy because most downtown areas across the country were suffering from high crime rates, deteriorating schools, worsening traffic congestion, and several other problems. The suburbs offered freedom from such woes.

Attached or Detached?

Perhaps the biggest decision you'll face as you begin shopping for a home is whether you want a freestanding detached house or an attached home (such as a condominium, co-op, or town house). Both types of housing have their advantages and drawbacks.

Freestanding detached homes are still favored by most buyers. They usually offer more privacy (and generally more peace and quiet) than condos or other kinds of attached homes, in part because there's more distance between neighbors. Buying a freestanding house also means you'll get a yard, a garage or carport, and a few other niceties that attached homes typically don't offer. On the downside, you probably won't have access to a pool, hot tub, and the host of other recreational amenities that many condo and town house projects offer their residents. Owning a freestanding house also means you'll spend lots of your own time keeping the property looking nice. In condo developments and other types of attached projects, maintenance duties are the responsibility of a local homeowners association—a group of residents that sets and enforces rules that everyone in the development must follow.

Many first-time buyers purchase a condo or other type of attached home because they usually cost tens of thousands of dollars less than freestanding homes that are similar in size. But it's important to realize that a lender will take into account the monthly payments you'll have to make to the homeowners association and thus lower the amount of money it will lend you. For example, a bank might preapprove you for a $180,000 mortgage to buy a freestanding house but only a $150,000 loan if you decide to purchase a condo or other type of attached home in a development where the owners must pay hefty monthly fees to a local homeowners association.

Things are different today. Many of the downtown areas that buyers once shunned—including those in Los Angeles, San Diego, Denver, Chicago, Baltimore, and St. Louis, to name a few—are enjoying a renaissance of sorts, drawing people back to their neighborhoods and pushing property values higher. Many of those downtown buyers are coming from the suburbs, which are now suffering growing pains of their own.

Your decision to buy in a downtown neighborhood or in an outlying suburb depends on several factors. One key item to consider is affordability: Will you get more house for your money downtown or do the suburbs offer a better deal? The best way to find out is to visit open houses in both areas and bring your completed "wants versus needs" checklist with you.

As you tour each property, think about how long it would take to commute from the home to your job. You might be willing to settle for a smaller place if it's close to your work, allowing more time to spend with your family or to pursue other interests. Conversely, spending an hour or two commuting each day won't matter much if you insist on living in a particular neighborhood or if the homes near your workplace don't meet your requirements—or your budget.

Restrictions

About one of three Americans now live in a community that's supervised by a homeowners association or similar group of residents who make and enforce rules that everyone who lives in the development must follow. Though associations were once used almost exclusively at condominium and co-op projects, a growing number of tracts that feature single-family homes are also governed by a homeowners group.

A reasonable set of rules can make living in a development more enjoyable. Having an association can even help push property values higher by ensuring that all homeowners keep their property in good shape and respect their neighbors' rights. But you'll definitely want to avoid buying a home in such a community if the association has more rules than a dog has fleas or if you're a firm believer that you should be able to do whatever you want with your home (or in it) as long as you don't break any laws.

You should also realize that almost all homeowners associations charge their residents a monthly fee: an important consideration if you expect your budget to be tight in your first few years of home ownership.

The Importance of Good Schools

No matter where you buy, it's important to remember that the quality of local schools will have a dramatic impact on the price you must pay and the profit you'll make when you eventually sell. Even if you don't have school-age children, the people who eventually buy your property probably will. All things being equal, parents are almost always willing to pay more for a home that's served by above-average schools.

Of course, the importance of buying in an area that features good schools should be obvious if you have school-age children of your own. Many first-time buyers make the mistake of thinking they can buy in a neighborhood that's served by a lousy school because they send their own kids to private school. But they rarely save money in the long run because the money they pay for tuition could instead be used to buy a home in a nicer neighborhood where the public schools are just fine.

Consider this: When mortgage rates are at 8 percent, every $1,000 you spend on tuition or other items (like a car loan or credit card debt) reduces your borrowing power by about $10,000. If you spend $6,000 per year in tuition, your mortgage borrowing power will be slashed by $60,000. You'd probably be a lot happier using the $6,000 to borrow an extra $60,000, which would allow you to buy a bigger house in a nice area where the public schools are good enough for your children to attend.

You'll learn how to determine quickly the quality of the public schools in the neighborhoods you visit in chapter 4. For now, all you need to remember is that you should never purchase a home in an area where schools "don't make the grade."

Cleaning Up Your Credit

Money might make the world go around, but credit is the grease that'll help you squeeze into your first home. It's imperative to get a copy of your credit report now,

before you earnestly begin looking for a home, so you'll have time to clear up any errors on the report before you submit your loan application.

Checking your credit file and fixing any mistakes is important for several reasons:

- *Credit bureaus make mistakes.* One recent study found that one-third of Americans have enough inaccurate information in their credit files to prevent them from getting a mortgage or other large loan. You might think your credit record is perfect but there's a good chance the files at the credit bureau contain errors that make you look like a bad credit risk. Federal law says you, not the bureau or a creditor, are responsible for maintaining an accurate credit history and correcting any mistakes.

- *Correcting errors takes time.* It'll take at least a week or two to make even the smallest "fix," such as updating your address or having a long-closed account deleted from your file. It could take several weeks or even a few months to make a major change, such as proving your payments are up-to-date on an account the credit bureau says is delinquent.

- *Lenders hate surprises.* Say you don't get a credit report now and instead wait for the bank to order the report after you file your mortgage application. If the report contains errors, the lender might automatically reject your loan request because it mistakenly believes that you're a bad credit risk or that you're trying to hide a checkered past. At best, the bank will make you correct the errors—which will result in lengthy and potentially costly processing delays that might even jeopardize your purchase.

It's also important to realize that the size of the loan you can get—as well as the interest rate and fees you'll be charged—will depend largely on your credit history. If you can present a lender with a sterling credit report, you'll likely be rewarded with a sizable loan and a rock-bottom interest rate. You'll be charged a higher rate if your credit record is only so-so, and you'll really pay through the nose if your report is worse than so-so. Every step you take to improve your credit profile now can increase your borrowing power while saving you hundreds or even thousands of dollars down the road.

First Steps toward Cleaner Credit

The first thing you need to do is to order a copy of your credit report from each of the "big three" nationwide credit reporting bureaus: Experian/TRW (888-397-3742), Equifax (800-685-1111), or Trans Union Corp. (800-888-4213). Each report will cost about $8.

When you receive each report, first make sure all the "basics" are correct—including the spelling of your name, your address, and your Social Security number. Then look at each credit account or loan that's listed on the report to ensure all the account numbers, outstanding balances, credit limits, and past-payment information (especially the number of delinquencies) are accurate.

Next, double-check the "opening dates" of the accounts. Mortgage lenders like to see at least one or two up-to-date accounts that have been open for at least a few years. You'll miss a golden opportunity to impress the lender with your creditworthiness if an account has been in good standing for five years but the credit bureau mistakenly believes it's been open for only five months—or has no record of the account at all.

VISIT THE WEB

Each of the "big three" credit bureaus has its own Web site that allows you to purchase a copy of your credit report online. Our favorite is operated by Experian/TRW (http://www.experian.com) because it features lots of "extras," including a biweekly question-and-answer column and an extensive database of credit-related information that you can access for free. The other two nationwide bureaus are Trans Union Corp. (http://www.transunion.com) and Equifax (http://www.equifax.com).

Also pay attention to how the bureau reports information about loans that you have paid off or credit accounts that you have voluntarily closed. If your report merely says "account closed," the lender you eventually ask for a home loan might mistakenly think it was ordered closed by the creditor—not you—because you refused to pay your debts. Your closed accounts should instead carry a notation such as "closed by customer" or "closed by account holder."

Understanding Your Rights

After you've eyeballed your report, it's time to request any necessary corrections. The federal Fair Credit Reporting Act (FCRA) requires a credit bureau to respond to your written request for a correction no later than 30 days after the request is received. But remember, there's a big difference between taking action to settle a dispute and actually resolving it. If the credit bureau gets your letter, sits on it for four weeks, and then forwards it to the original creditor for comment, the bureau will have met its legal obligation to respond to your request within 30 days even though several more weeks may pass before the issue is resolved and your report is corrected. That's just one more reason why you need to start cleaning up your record now instead of waiting until you've picked out a house and filed a mortgage application.

Requesting Corrections

All credit bureaus require that you put virtually any request for a correction in writing. Your request must be sent to the bureau's address, which you'll find at the bottom of your credit report or on the reverse side of the report's final page. Here are some tips to follow, whether you're using the bureau's own dispute form or writing your letter from scratch:

- *Make sure you clearly identify which item(s) you are disputing.* Some of the information on your credit report might be wrong but the majority will be correct. Your letter must specifically state which items need correction, and why. The FCRA allows credit bureaus to automatically reject vague or "blanket" requests, such as a one-sentence letter stating, "There are inaccuracies in my report that must be corrected."

- *Include any evidence that supports your request for a correction.* Copies of canceled checks, credit card statements, and cash receipts are just a few of the documents you can submit as proof that a bill was paid on time or an account was closed while it was still in good standing. If the creditor that's subsequently contacted by the credit bureau can't refute your evidence or simply doesn't respond to the query, the bureau must automatically wipe the negative information off your record.

- *Use buzzwords to grab the credit bureau's attention.* Keep your correction request brief (no more than a page or two) but also make sure it includes the term *dispute* or *challenge* at least once or twice. A rambling letter that doesn't clearly identify a specific problem will be set aside until an overworked customer service rep or clerk finally has time to read it and attempt to figure out what you want.

- *Be clear about the action you want the credit bureau to take.* If you can provide evidence that damaging information on your report is wrong, specifically state that you want the delinquency or other mistake deleted from your record. Similarly, make sure that any account you closed at your own volition is marked "closed by consumer" rather than merely "closed." You don't want the mortgage lender to think your credit was shut off because you didn't make your payments.

VISIT THE WEB

AOL's credit information center (http://www. creditinfocenter.com) has lots of useful material, including advice from consumer advocates and lawyers as well as sample letters you can use to dispute errors on your credit report.

It's a good idea to send your request to the credit bureau via certified mail. The receipt you'll receive a week later could be useful if the bureau later claims it never received your letter and documentation.

The Bureau's Obligations

Again, the FCRA requires a credit bureau to respond to a consumer's request within 30 days. If you've made a simple request that requires little or no investigation—such as correcting the spelling of your name or updating your address—the matter can be resolved in a matter of days. But it could easily take a month or two if the bureau must contact one of your current or past creditors before your file can be updated.

The FCRA requires the bureau to send you a written notice of its findings no later than five days after its investigation is completed. If you win the dispute, you'll also receive a new copy of your credit report showing the changes that have been made.

But what if you lose? You'll still have a few options. First, you can demand a reinvestigation if the creditor that the bureau contacted responded with inaccurate or erroneous information. Or you can take the matter up directly with the creditor, using your arsenal of canceled checks and previous statements to prove that the creditor's files are incorrect. If the creditor finally agrees with you, insist that it send a letter to all of the bureaus it uses stating that the damaging information should be removed from your file. Make sure the creditor sends you a copy of the letter for your own files.

If you can't persuade the creditor or credit bureau to erase the black mark on your record, the FCRA gives you the right to add a 100-word letter to your file that explains your version of the dispute. The letter will become a permanent part of your record and will be attached to any credit report a mortgage lender or other prospective creditor obtains about you in the future.

It's important to write such a letter if the dispute isn't resolved in your favor and you earnestly believe that you're right and the stubborn creditor is wrong. The letter will ensure that your side of the story will be considered when you apply for a loan to buy your first home. It might also earn you some "brownie points" with the bank: Lenders feel more confident about borrowers who understand the importance of maintaining the best possible credit rating, and the fact that you took the time to put your version in writing will indicate you're serious about maintaining a good credit profile.

Special Credit Issues for First-Time Buyers

Mortgage lenders feel better about making a loan when the applicant has a long credit history that goes back several years. But many first-time buyers don't have much of a history at all, especially if they're relatively young or don't make the big bucks that prompt credit card companies to aggressively court their business. Here are some tips to help you establish a solid credit history, which will ultimately improve your chances of obtaining a mortgage:

- *Get credit where credit's due.* Most landlords, telephone companies, utilities, and the like don't report your payment information to credit bureaus unless you're seriously behind on your bills. If you have a good payment history with them, ask them to begin reporting your information to the "big three" credit bureaus. It's a good way to fatten up your credit history.

- *Keep payments on all your existing credit cards or loans current.* Lenders aren't overly concerned about a handful of late payments made by someone with a long and otherwise stellar credit record. But the impact of just one or two "lates" can be dramatic if you're a first-time buyer whose credit history only goes back a few years.

- *Pay down your outstanding balances.* Mortgage lenders are wary of first-time buyers who have incurred a lot of debt, fearing they won't be able to handle the even larger payments required by a mortgage. Whittling down the balances on your credit cards or other debts will improve your chances of gaining loan approval and allow you to qualify for a bigger mortgage to buy a better home.

- *If you don't have any credit cards, apply for one or two.* Ask for a relatively small credit limit, no more than $2,000. Use the cards to make a few modest purchases each month and then promptly pay most or all of their outstanding balances when the statements arrive. If you can't get a conventional credit card, you can get a "secured" card from a bank in exchange for agreeing to open a special savings account.

- *Don't change jobs now.* Many first-time buyers don't realize that frequently changing jobs can ultimately hurt their chances of getting a mortgage. Lenders often feel several changes indicate that the prospective borrower is flighty or simply incapable of holding a job. So don't change jobs now unless you're offered a better-paying position that's in the same line of work that you're doing today.

Top Five Things to Do Right Now

1. Fill out the "wants versus needs" checklist. It'll help you keep your housing priorities straight when you start looking for your first home.

2. Order a copy of your credit report from each of the "big three" credit reporting bureaus. There's a good chance they contain errors, even if you believe your record is spotless.

3. Read each credit report carefully. Remember, even the slightest error could greatly affect the amount of money a mortgage lender will let you borrow or the rate that you will be charged.

4. Immediately dispute any erroneous information on your reports that hurt your credit rating. If you instead wait until you apply for a mortgage or make an offer on a house, you'll subject yourself to costly delays because each dispute could take several weeks to resolve.

5. If you can't get a damaging piece of information removed, exercise your right to include a 100-word letter in your permanent credit file that tells your side of the story. The letter will ensure your version of the events surrounding the damaging data will be considered when you eventually apply for a mortgage.

ON Your Mark, Get SET . . .

CHAPTER THREE

You're almost ready to begin shopping for a home. But before you do, there are a few more important decisions you must make.

After you've started polishing your credit record by following the steps in the previous chapter, there's really only two more things to do before you're ready to hit the streets in search of your new home. First, you have to determine exactly how much cash you have available to make a down payment and cover your transaction-related closing costs. And second—assuming you're like most first-time buyers—you'll need to find a real estate agent who makes you confident that you'll get the best possible home at the lowest possible price.

Raising a Down Payment

So, how much money do you have available to make a down payment on your first home? Do you have $5,000? Maybe $10,000? Have you been able to squirrel away $20,000, $40,000, or more?

You'd be surprised at the number of first-time buyers who don't really know how much they can afford to "put down" on a house. Some buyers underestimate their down payment power by simply totaling the balances of their checking and savings accounts—inadvertently ignoring tens of thousands of additional dollars they might have in stocks, a retirement plan, or other investments that can be tapped for a down payment. On the flip side, many first-time buyers overestimate the amount of cash they have for a down payment because they don't understand how transaction-related "closing costs" can take a huge bite out of the money they have saved to buy a home.

Understanding Closing Costs

Technically, a real estate deal involves only two parties: a seller who offers a house and a buyer who agrees to purchase it. But in reality there are typically a dozen or so other people involved in a sale—including realty agents, inspectors, insurance representatives, and an escrow officer or closing attorney who'll oversee all the paperwork. All of them will expect to be paid on the day the sale closes or perhaps even sooner.

The fees you must pay to these professionals will comprise a big chunk of your closing costs. Closing costs are transaction-related expenses that are charged whenever a property changes hands. It's not unusual for closing costs to cover 15, 20, or even more than 30 different items.

In addition to the fees you must pay to the various professionals involved in the sale, another major piece of your closing costs will involve charges levied by the lender who agrees to finance your purchase. The biggest lender-related charge will likely be for the points you must pay to get a mortgage. One point is equal to 1 percent of your total loan amount: If you need a $140,000 loan and the lender charges three points, the total cost of your points will be $4,200.

The more points you agree to pay, the lower the rate on your mortgage will be. For example, a lender might offer you a 7.5 percent rate if you pay three points, a 7.75 percent rate if you only want to pay two points, or an 8 percent rate if you pay only one point. Many lenders offer loans with no points at all, although they make up for it by charging you an even higher interest rate.

We'll discuss the advantages and disadvantages of paying points in more detail in chapter 7. For now, you just need to remember two things: (1) the number of points you agree to pay will have a dramatic effect on your total closing costs, and (2) you probably will want to choose a loan with no points (even though your interest rate over the life of the loan will be higher) if you don't have a lot of cash and thus need to keep your closing costs as low as possible.

Everything's Negotiable

There are a couple of other things you need to understand about closing costs. First, who has to pay them—the buyer or the seller—is negotiable. For example, the buyer usually winds up paying the $200 to $400 fee levied by a home inspector and the $75 or so charge to have the sale recorded at the government recorder's office. But there's no reason why your offer can't request that the seller pay them. The worst thing that can happen is that you'll be told "no."

Your chances of getting the seller to pick up most or all of the closing costs will largely depend on the strength of the local housing market. Your request will stand a much better chance of being accepted if sales are slow and the seller is anxious to make a deal. Conversely, you might need to pay for the lion's share of closing costs if the seller has several other offers on the table and most of them are near the asking price.

Sorry, Cash Only

In a typical sale, you can expect your share of the closing costs to equal around 5 or 6 percent of the home's purchase price. The seller's share will likely equal about 10 percent, including a sales commission for the help of a salesperson. On a $100,000 home, your share of the closing costs would likely be between $5,000 and $6,000. On a $150,000 home, figure on spending about $9,000.

ROLL 'EM

Some lenders will allow you to roll most of your closing costs into your total loan amount, essentially letting you pay the costs off over 30 years instead of paying for them up front. It's an option worth considering, especially if you don't have a lot of cash now and you'll need every penny you've saved to muster a down payment.

It's important to realize that closing costs almost always must be paid in cash. The bank will let you finance the purchase price over several years, but the inspectors and all the other people who work on the sale will want to be paid in full when they render their services or on the day the deal closes. As a result, the closing costs you pay will eat up a sizable portion of the money you've been hoping to use for a down payment.

Let's say you've scraped together $12,000 and plan to use the money to make a 10 percent down payment on a $120,000 house. If your closing costs will equal 6 percent of your purchase price, $7,200 of your $12,000 will be chewed up by your closing expenses—meaning that you'll have only $4,800 (or 4 percent of you home's price) left for a down payment. Many lenders are willing to loan you money if you can make a 10 percent down payment. Far fewer will give you a loan if you're putting just 4 percent down.

The lesson here is that you have to anticipate your closing costs and then budget accordingly. If you're working with a real estate agent, the agent can give you a fairly good estimate of what your closing costs will be. If you aren't using an agent, you can use the 6-percent-of-your-expected-purchase-price guideline to get a ballpark idea of your closing costs.

The lender will give you a written, good faith estimate of your closing costs a few days after you apply for a mortgage. Trouble is, if the estimate is far more than you expected, you won't have much time to scrape together enough cash to cover the shortfall. That's another reason why you need to estimate your closing costs now, before you earnestly begin looking for a home. It's the only way to ensure that you'll have enough cash set aside to pay all those expenses on closing day, when the final papers are signed and you get the keys to your new home.

Your Down Payment

You don't need a truckload of money to buy a house, but you must have *some*. Many lenders will give you a loan if you can make a down payment equal to 5 percent of the home's purchase price, especially if you qualify for the popular Federal Housing Administration (FHA) mortgage plan or are willing to accept an adjustable-rate mortgage instead of a fixed-rate loan. You'll have many more borrowing options if you can make at least a 10 percent down payment. And if you can muster a down payment of 20 percent or more, you should be able to take your pick from a variety of different plans and may even qualify for the lowest possible interest rate.

We'll talk more about your mortgage options in chapter 7. For now, all you need to know is that your chances of gaining loan approval rise with every dollar you commit toward a down payment.

There are a couple of reasons why lenders generally prefer loan applicants who make large down payments over those who make small ones. First, studies have consistently shown that people who make large down payments are far less likely to default—to quit paying—than are buyers who make the smallest down payment possible. And second, making a large down payment means you won't have to borrow as much money, which in turn means your monthly housing payments will take a smaller bite out of your paycheck and further reduce the chances that you'll default.

The worksheet on page 38 will help you get a handle on how much cash you've got available to make a down payment. Of course, just because the money is available doesn't mean you have to use it all. For example, you might want to make a relatively small down payment if you need to keep some cash tucked away to pay an upcoming college tuition bill or to meet unexpected expenses. You might also want to make the smallest down payment possible if it will free up some money to make other investments or to start a retirement plan.

Ultimately, the lender will determine the minimum down payment you can make and still qualify for the loan you need. You're free to add as much as you like on top of that minimum amount if you're fortunate enough to have some excess cash.

How Much 'Ya Got?

Spending a few minutes to complete this worksheet will give you a good idea of how much cash you have available to make a down payment and pay for closing costs. Simply fill in the blanks (and the blanks for your coborrower if a spouse or someone else is buying the home with you). You don't have to use all of your available cash to buy a home but it helps to know exactly how much you've got at your disposal.

Source	You	Coborrower
1. Cash in checking and savings accounts. Also include money market funds and short-term certificates of deposit.	$ _____	$ _____
2. Other liquid assets. Include longer-term CDs and stocks, bonds, or other investments that can easily be sold.	$ _____	$ _____
3. Gift funds. This is the total amount of any money that your folks or other people have promised to give you.	$ _____	$ _____
4. Retirement savings. You can withdraw or borrow against your nest egg but discuss the tax implications with an accountant first.	$ _____	$ _____
5. Home sale proceeds. If you're selling a home first, estimate your net proceeds after the mortgage is paid off and any commissions or other closing costs are paid.	$ _____	$ _____
Subtotals	$ _____	$ _____
Total Cash Available		$ _____

Getting the Cash for Your Down Payment

The biggest obstacle most first-time buyers face is raising enough money to make a down payment. You'll need to be creative as you think about different ways to scrape together the cash. You'll also want to stretch your available dollars as far as they can go. You can probably take advantage of at least a few of the following possibilities:

- Ask your parents, other relatives, or friends for help. If they can't give or loan you any money, perhaps they'll agree to cosign your application to improve your chances of getting a mortgage.

- Get a second job and set the earnings aside for a down payment. You can quit after you buy a home and move in, provided you earn enough from your primary job to meet your new mortgage obligations.

- Raise your tax withholding allowances to the legal limit so you'll keep more of your gross pay. The extra cash can be added to your down payment savings, while the tax breaks you'll get by purchasing the house should help you break even on April 15.

- Buy a home with a friend. The two of you could split the down payment, tax deductions, and eventual resale profits. You'd also improve your chances of getting a mortgage because lenders figure that two incomes are better than one.

- Look for an outside investor. The investor could make some or all of the down payment, you could make the monthly payments, and the two of you could split the profits when the home is sold.

- Sell securities you own or borrow against them with the help of your stockbroker.

- Sell a boat, RV, or second car you may own or borrow against them and use the proceeds for a down payment.

- Sell your collectibles or heirlooms. You'd be surprised how much your old baseball cards or grandma's broach might fetch.

- Pawn something you own, and use the money for the down payment. You can buy the item back after you move in.

- Withdraw money from your individual retirement account (IRA) or similar plan. A law that took effect in 1998 removed the traditional 10 percent early withdrawal penalty for first-time homebuyers.

- Borrow against your retirement funds. The interest rate on the loan could be as low as 2 or 3 percent.

- Cash in the built-up value of your life insurance or borrow against it. Your insurer can provide the details.

- Ask your church, synagogue, or other nonprofit group for help. Many offer assistance to first-time buyers.

- Ask about leasing the property with an option to buy, known as a *lease-option,* to rent the home now and buy it later, after you've had more time to save for a down payment.

- Check out government loans that require little cash. The Federal Housing Administration lets you buy with as little as 5 percent down, or even a mere 3 percent if prices in the area are extremely low. The Veterans Administration offers programs for veterans that require absolutely nothing down.

- Offer something other than cash as a down payment. Sellers have been known to accept cars, jewelry, and even small businesses in lieu of a cash down payment.

- Provide services instead of cash. Contractors, secretaries, even young lawyers and doctors have bought their first home by offering the seller a few hundred hours of their services instead of making a cash down payment.

- Ask the seller to carryback a second mortgage. Every dollar the seller agrees to take in installments will knock $1 off the cash you need to close the deal.

- Look for foreclosed homes. Some lenders and government agencies will let you buy their foreclosures with little or nothing down, especially if your credit is good and they're anxious to get the home occupied.

Working with a Real Estate Agent

Christopher Columbus wouldn't have discovered America without the help of his trusty mapmaker. Astronaut Neil Armstrong couldn't have taken that first step on the moon if he didn't have Mission Control guiding him along the way. And as a first-time homebuyer, you'll probably need a real estate agent at your side as you set sail on your homebuying journey and try to navigate from a purchase offer to a successful closing.

Good real estate agents are worth their weight in gold. The agent will help you find the best available property that's in your price range and then negotiate on your behalf to get the best deal. Once your offer is accepted, the agent will then guide the transaction down the road to a successful close—a road that's filled with more potholes than Jed Clampett's old farm. An agent's negotiating skills, real estate connections, knowledge of the local housing market, and even contract law can save you literally hundreds of hours and thousands of dollars.

Alas, not all agents are good agents. More than one million people across the nation sell real estate, either part-time or full-time. Many of them know even less about the business than you do. The next few pages will show you how to sort through all the salespeople who are clamoring for your business and pick the one who's best for you.

VISIT THE WEB

The National Association of REALTORS® Web site (http://www.realtor.com) has lots of useful information about buying and selling a home, more than one million property listings, and a search function to help you locate agents who work in your area.

How Agents Are Paid

In most real estate transactions, the seller—not the buyer—is responsible for paying for the agent's services. In a typical scenario, the home-

owner hires a *seller's agent* to market the home on a commission basis. When the sale closes, the seller's agent is paid a commission equal to about 6 percent of the sales price. If the buyer was represented by a different agent, the seller's agent gives the buyer's agent half of the commission. In short, the buyer pays *absolutely nothing* for all the help the agent provided.

Sounds like a sweet deal for the buyer, eh? Sometimes it is, but other times it isn't. Be especially wary if you're dealing directly with the seller's agent instead of using an agent of your own. When it comes down to brass tacks, the agent will be paid by the seller—which means (in most states) that the law essentially requires the agent to put the seller's best interests ahead of yours.

Now, don't start feeling like the home-sales game is rigged against the buyer. It isn't. Even though the agent may be paid by the seller, the agent also has a duty to represent you as best as legally possible. Most important, this means the salesperson can't lie to you, keep secrets from you concerning possible construction defects the seller has privately acknowledged, or pull any other shenanigans. Doing so can get the agent banned from the business, possibly thrown in jail, and allow you to file one hellacious lawsuit for damages. So, a good agent will work hard for you even if it's the seller who'll ultimately pay for the agent's services.

Protecting Yourself

Most buyers aren't overly concerned with the tiny nuances of the laws that guide an agent's professional behavior. You shouldn't lose sleep over them, either. But if you're uncomfortable, you have two options to provide yourself with some extra protection.

The first choice is to trust the agent you're dealing with, but make sure you don't tell that agent more than he or she really needs to know. For example, when you find a home you like, you obviously need to tell your agent how much you want to offer so that a formal bid can be prepared and submitted to the seller. But it would be foolish to say something like, "I want the initial offer to be for $135,000, but I'm willing to go as high as $150,000 if it's rejected." In some states, the agent would have to disclose your secret to the seller, thus wiping out all your negotiating power.

Your second (and probably safest) choice is to hire an agent or broker who is legally required to represent you and *only* you. There are now more than 200,000 of these so-called "buyer's brokers" or "buyer's agents" who will negotiate exclusively with your best interests in mind. Anything you tell a buyer's broker must stay with the broker and cannot be shared with the seller or the seller's agent.

The Buyer's Broker

Using a buyer's broker can provide you with some much needed peace of mind. It can also (but not always) result in paying the lowest possible price for a home or getting other valuable concessions from the seller.

The drawback, of course, is that you have to pay for the broker's services yourself. Some brokers work for a flat fee, regardless of how long it takes to help you find a home or how much you agree to pay for it. Others work on a commission basis, much like the way a seller's agent is paid. Still others charge an hourly rate or a basic retainer fee that can be raised if finding a home and closing the deal takes an inordinate amount of the broker's time.

Before you hire a buyer's broker, you obviously need to know the cost of the services that will be rendered. It's also important to realize that the typical buyer's broker contract will require that you pay the broker a fee even if you wind up finding a house on your own or with the help of a different agent.

Though you're technically responsible for paying for a buyer's broker's services, there's no reason why you can't try to recover those costs when you make an offer on the home you want to buy. For example, say you make an offer on a $100,000 house that the sellers have listed with their own agent. The sellers' agent would have to share half of the 6 percent commission with the agent who produces a buyer. Your offer could stipulate that the sellers' agent share the commission with your buyer's broker, eliminating the need to pay the broker yourself. The sellers and their agent wouldn't lose any money because the sellers were expecting to pay a 6 percent commission anyway and the sellers' agent was expecting to share half that check with the buyer's agent. Meantime, your buyer's broker would be paid in full even though you didn't have to take a nickel out of your own pocket.

Choosing an Agent

Do You Really Need an Agent?

Most buyers, especially those who have never purchased a home before, need to enlist the help of a good real estate agent. Don't even consider buying a home without an agent unless you meet the standards below.

- *You have plenty of time on your hands.* A good agent will look at all the available properties for you, filter out those that don't fit your needs and price range, and help you arrange visits to the most promising homes. It will require dozens or even hundreds of hours of your time to do the work yourself.

- *You're up-to-date on local home prices.* With a few computer keystrokes, real estate agents can access important (and sometimes confidential) records about recent home sales that can determine whether a seller's asking price presents a great bargain or is far too high. Don't go it alone unless you're privy to the same information.

- *You're an expert negotiator.* An agent can use knowledge of local sales trends and negotiating expertise to get a price discount or wring other valuable concessions from the seller. You can do it too, but only if you're armed with the proper information and have the temperament needed to deal with a seller who might make outlandish demands.

- *You know other experts to help you complete the sale.* Even if you're willing to look for a home yourself and personally handle the negotiations, you'll need to form a team of other professionals—an inspector, a title insurer, an escrow holder, and the like—to complete the transaction. A good agent will already have a network of reliable service providers in place.

- *You're ready to take responsibility if the sale goes awry.* Working without an agent means you're willing to assume sole responsibility if you screw-up—such as forgetting to have the home inspected for hidden defects or losing your deposit because you couldn't find a lender to finance the

transaction. Using an agent will minimize the chances of making such mistakes and may even allow you to seek reimbursement from the agent's company if the transaction falls apart.

Choosing a good real estate agent or buyer's broker isn't too difficult but it will take at least three or four hours of your time. You need to compile an initial list of ten or so candidates, and then spend about ten minutes on the phone with each of them to narrow your list of finalists down to three or four. When you've got your handful of finalists, you need to sit down with each of them for a half hour or so to ask some probing questions and then spend an equal amount of time calling their references before you make a final decision.

Sure, you're probably busy and anxious to start looking for your first home. But spending a few hours now to find the best agent will pay huge dividends down the road. Choosing the wrong agent could mean wasting weeks of your time looking at properties that don't fit your needs or paying far too much for a home that a good agent would have instantly recognized as being overpriced.

BE SELECTIVE

Too many first-time buyers make the mistake of simply choosing the agent who's always sending them newsletters or passing out cheap freebies such as notepads or refrigerator magnets. Every agent knows how to put a stamp on a newsletter or print a notepad but it doesn't necessarily mean you should trust that agent to help you buy a home—one of the biggest investments that you'll make in your life.

Finding Prospective Candidates

The first step you must take to find the agent that's best for you is to compile a "starting list" of ten or so candidates. Here are some tips to help you compile your initial list:

- *Ask neighbors and coworkers for recommendations.* Pay particular attention to referrals made by friends who bought a home within the past 12 months and were happy with the service their agent provided. Your accountant, lawyer, or other professionals you trust are also good sources of referrals.

- *Visit open houses in the neighborhoods that interest you.* Such visits give you a chance to meet local agents and see how they interact with prospective buyers. Get the agents' business cards and add the names of those that most impressed you to your initial list of prospects.

- *Attend free homebuying seminars.* Many lenders, real estate organizations, and individual brokerage companies offer free or low-cost workshops for first-time buyers. They're a great opportunity to meet agents, not to mention build your "buyer IQ."

- *Go ahead—call the agent who always seems to be knocking on your door.* Again, you shouldn't automatically chose the agent who has given you the most pot holders or other little chotchkies. But the fact that the agent is always in the neighborhood probably means that agent knows a lot about the local market, which is a particularly valuable asset if you expect to purchase a home in the same area that you live in now.

Narrowing Your List

After you've compiled a list of roughly ten agents, call each one to conduct a brief telephone interview. You shouldn't need to spend more than five or ten minutes on the phone with each one to determine if they should be included among the three or four agents who you'll ask to meet with in person.

When you make each call, tell the agent a little bit about yourself and your homebuying plans. Give high marks to the agents who listen attentively, ask a few questions themselves, and seem genuinely interested in helping you buy your first home. Scratch the agent's name off your list of potential finalists if that agent doesn't seem to be listening to you, is constantly putting your call on hold to talk to someone else, or simply doesn't seem to know very much about the neighborhoods that interest you.

Also make sure to ask each agent whether he or she works full-time or part-time. It's usually best to choose a full-time agent, because keeping abreast of the real estate market to quickly spot the best deals (not to mention servicing you) is a full-time job. If you hire a part-timer, you're essentially agreeing that the demands of that agent's

full-time job are more important than helping you buy your first home.

The Final Four

After phoning the ten or so agents on your initial list of candidates, you should have a pretty good idea which three or four salespeople are worth spending your time to meet with in person. Some of your finalists may suggest meeting with you in your current home or perhaps over coffee at a local restaurant.

It's important for you to politely decline such offers and instead insist that you meet in the agent's own office. Visiting the agent's office will give you a chance to check out the company that agent works for, which speaks volumes about the agent and the amount of office support available. A good agent works in a well-kept and well-organized office, staffed with other courteous and professional people. You don't want to hire an agent who works in a place that looks like it was hit by a tornado, where nobody picks up a ringing telephone, and the person in charge of running the operation smells of alcohol or hasn't been seen in days.

DEMAND COURTESY

If an agent that you're thinking about hiring doesn't return your telephone call by the next morning, delete that agent's name from your list of candidates. If an agent can't find time to talk to you now, that agent is either too busy with other clients or just too lazy to deserve your business.

Ask the Right Questions

After you have narrowed your list of potential agent-candidates down to three or four, you need to schedule personal interviews with each of the finalists in their office. Asking the important questions below will help you choose the agent who's best for you.

- *Do you work full-time or part-time?* If you forgot to ask the agent this question when you first called, make sure you do it now. It's best to choose a full-time agent because staying abreast of the market, quickly spotting the best deals, and shepherding a sale to a successful close is a full-time job.

- *How long have you been selling real estate?* It's generally best to work with an agent who has at least two or three years of experience. Let the rookies learn on some other buyer's time.

- *How many other buyers and sellers are you working with now?* A good agent often works with between five and twelve clients at a time. Any less could be a sign that the agent isn't very aggressive. Working with more than 12 or 15 customers may mean the agent is too busy to focus on your home-buying needs.

- *Do you hold any professional designations?* The industry awards special titles to agents who've completed in-depth training courses and passed grueling tests. A long list of titles is no guarantee that the agent is a "winner," but at least shows that agent takes the job seriously by staying on top of industry trends.

- *What kind of office support do you have?* A growing number of real estate firms now employ behind-the-scenes specialists to handle everything from transaction-related paperwork to legal questions that might arise. It's certainly better to work with an agent who has lots of support than with an agent who must do everything alone.

- *How much do you know about me?* You shouldn't be sitting down with the agent now if you haven't already had one or two brief conversations about the type of home you're looking for, your price range, and the like. If the agent didn't bother taking notes or can't remember what you said, it may be a sign of disorganization or disinterest in getting your business.

- *Can I have a list of all the transactions you've worked on over the past 12 months?* Make sure the list includes property addresses, sales prices, and the names of the buyers or sellers the agent represented. Call three or four buyers listed on the sheet to see if they were happy with the agent's services. Beware of agents who won't give you such a list; salespeople with a thick dossier of happy clients are always pleased to provide referrals.

- *Is there anything else I should know about you or your company?* This catchall question gives you a chance to glean some important last-minute information. For example, one agent confided to a California couple that he was about to embark on a six-week European vacation. Despite the salesman's promises that he could handle their business on a long-distance basis, the couple wisely chose a different agent who could immediately help them start shopping for a home.

It's imperative that agents provide you with a list of all their transactions over the past 12 months and the name of the person they represented in each deal so you can check the agents' references. A good agent may have worked on 20, 30, or even more than 50 sales over the past year. Obviously, you don't have time to contact each of their previous clients to ask how satisfied they were with the services the agent provided. You can probably limit your reference checking to about six calls per agent by following these tips:

- Don't bother calling any sellers who appear on the agent's list of previous clients. You're a buyer, which means you have a totally different set of needs than someone who recently sold a home or is trying to sell their property now.

- Only call buyers who purchased a home that's in your current price range or neighborhood. As a first-time buyer, you're probably looking for a home that's in a nice but affordable area. Calling a buyer who purchased a far more expensive property would likely be a waste of your time: The dynamics of the high-priced housing market are far different than those that rule more modest areas.

- Spread your calls out over clients the agent has served over different periods of time. Calling one or two buyers the agent helped 12 months ago, another one or two from six months ago, and two of the agent's more recent buyers will help you determine if the quality of the agent's service has remained consistent or has recently suffered due to some type of distraction (such as an office reorganization or personal problems).

In the end, you'll want to select an agent who demonstrates market knowledge, enthusiasm, a long list of previously satisfied clients, and the ability to make you feel comfortable when talking about your homebuying plans.

Top Five Things to Do Right Now

1. Use the "How Much 'Ya Got" worksheet to determine how much cash you have available to make a down payment and meet your closing costs.

2. Consider all the different ways to scrape together a down payment or to increase its size.

3. Decide if you want to use a real estate agent to help you buy a house or whether you'd feel more comfortable "flying solo."

4. If you decide to use an agent, compile a list of about ten potential candidates and narrow the list to three or four finalists by following the suggestions in this chapter.

5. Choose an agent based on that agent's responses to your questions, feedback you get from the agent's previous clients, and the agent's ability to make you feel comfortable when discussing your homebuying plans.

LET the (House) Hunt BEGIN!

CHAPTER FOUR

Finding the right house for you is basically a three-step process: find the best neighborhood you can afford, visit all the properties in the area to locate the best buys, and then focus your efforts on the one or two homes that you really like.

You've probably heard it a hundred times: The three most important things to consider when you're buying a home are "location, location, and location." Like most clichés, this old adage is filled with truisms—and is also somewhat misleading.

True, the location of the home you buy will play a big role in determining how happy you'll be while you live there. The neighborhood you choose will also have a huge impact on the profits you make when you sell. But buying a home that doesn't fit your needs or is loaded with defects is a surefire way to lose both money and sleep, even if the property is located in Beverly Hills or next door to Donald Trump's New York estate.

You certainly can find a home you like in a neighborhood you can afford—and vice versa—but it's going to take some time. First you have to target the two or three most promising neighborhoods, then visit all the properties for sale in those areas, and finally zero in on the two or three homes that are truly outstanding buys.

As your homebuying journey unfolds, remember to take your time. Don't set unrealistic deadlines for yourself and don't get pushed into signing a sales contract by an aggressive real estate agent or seller. Purchasing a home is one of the biggest financial and emotional commitments that you'll make in your entire life. Yet, you'd be surprised at the number of first-time buyers who decide to take a leisurely weekend drive, wind up visiting a few open houses "just for fun," and a few hours later find themselves writing a check for thousands of dollars to make a nonrefundable deposit on the first home they walked into. Any honest real estate agent who has been in business for a few years will admit that it happens all the time.

Avoiding Bad Investment Areas

When all's said and done, you expect the home you buy to increase in value. There's absolutely nothing wrong with having such expectations. After all, why would you possibly want to buy a house in a neighborhood where values are plummeting?

Yet, you'd be surprised at the number of otherwise intelligent first-time buyers who make that simple mistake. In a typical scenario, a newly married couple that's expecting to begin a family soon starts looking for a three-bedroom home in what they figure is a "pretty good" neighborhood. They soon discover that they can't possibly afford to buy a home that size in the community they have chosen, so they instead decide to look for a similar-sized home in an "average" neighborhood.

Guess what? They can't afford a three-bedroom house in that "average" neighborhood either. Rather than downsizing their expectations by looking for a smaller home in a good area, they wind up buying a three-bedroom house in a community that they don't really like. The public schools aren't very good, the guy down the street has a car parked in his yard, or maybe it's a little scary to walk their dog after the sun goes down. They figure such drawbacks aren't really important because

they'll eventually be able to sell their home for a nice profit and use the money to purchase a nicer house in a better neighborhood.

Fast-forward a few years. The couple's family is expanding, so it's time to move. But alas, the local schools have continued to deteriorate, several neighbors now have junked cars in their yard, and even driving to the local market for a quart of milk has become a harrowing experience. The couple's home is now worth a lot less than they paid for it because any buyer with a room temperature IQ isn't interested in purchasing in an area that's plagued with so many problems. If they're lucky, our beleaguered couple will break even after they sell and pay all their closing costs. But it's quite possible that they'll actually lose money and maybe even wind up owing the bank thousands of dollars. Either way, they'll have nothing left to purchase even the smallest home in a better neighborhood.

So, what did the buyers do wrong? They bought a house in the wrong neighborhood. Even the worst house can be restored to good-as-new condition. But it's impossible for you to personally "fix up" an entire community, and prices in an area that's declining are almost certain to continue dropping. A golden rule of homebuying is that you should always choose a neighborhood first and then look for the best home you can afford in the area you have selected—even if the home is smaller or in poorer condition than you'd like. Buying in an area where prices are tumbling can guarantee only one thing: heartbreak when it's time to sell.

Tracking Price Trends

It's imperative to buy in a neighborhood where prices have been rising for at least the past several months. It's even safer to limit your search to neighborhoods where values have risen for the past year. If your research shows that prices in your area are falling, seriously consider postponing your homebuying plans and use the time to pay off your debt and save more toward a down payment. Buying a house in an area where prices are dropping is a surefire way to lose money. A better idea would be to continue renting, update your research every few months, and then buy when the statistics you've gathered show that prices are rising again.

Getting the information you need to determine where values have been climbing and where they're falling isn't very difficult. You just have to remember that you can't automatically trust a real estate agent who says something like, "Oh, prices around here have been going up 5 or 10 percent a year" or sellers who swear their home "is worth twice as much as we paid for it a few years ago." You need proof that what they're saying is correct.

The CMA: A Buyer's Best Friend

A key to finding a neighborhood where prices are rising is to have a real estate agent prepare a written comparable market analysis (CMA) for each of the areas that interest you. Even if you have decided against working with an agent now, many agents will provide a complimentary CMA with the hope of landing your business in the future. Others will prepare a report for a flat fee of $50 or $100.

Different brokerage firms use different formats but a good CMA provides vital information about all the homes that have sold in the community over the past 6 to 12 months. The report should also provide similar information about all the homes that are for sale now. Many agents break their CMA reports down into two sections, one that covers homes that are currently for sale and one that focuses on properties that have already been sold. A sample of what a typical two-part CMA looks like is on pages 55–56.

Understanding the CMA

A comprehensive CMA may include a dozen or more listings of properties that are currently for sale and an equal number of transactions that have recently been completed. Looking at each entry and comparing the homes for sale section with the recent sales section can yield valuable information.

For example, note that all the homes listed in the recent sales section of our sample CMA fetched a higher price than each of the properties that were sold earlier. Importantly, all of those homes were roughly the same size and in roughly the same condition—meaning that they were truly "comparable" to each other. Rising "comps" are a sign that a neighborhood is on an upswing and merits closer attention.

What a Good CMA Looks Like

A good comparable market analysis will yield important clues about whether or not prices in a neighborhood are rising and which homes are the best bargains. Many real estate companies separate their CMA reports into two parts, the first for recent sales and the second for current listings. Here are some sample CMA entries for a fictitious neighborhood called Flowerwood:

Recent Sales: Flowerwood Area

CMA prepared by: John Bigbucks, Bigbucks Real Estate Co.
Date prepared: 02/05/99

Address:	123 Rose Ave.		
Date listed/Offering price:	12/05/98	$ 167,900	
Date sold/Sales price:	01/21/99	$ 164,000	
BRs/BA/Square feet:	3 BR	2 BA	1,760 SF

Comments: Good condition, remodeled kitchen, new built-ins.

Address:	145 Lilly Dr.		
Date listed/Offering price:	11/15/98	$ 167,000	
Date sold/Sales price:	01/15/99	$ 161,000	
BRs/BA/Square feet:	3 BR	2 BA	1,780 SF

Comments: Good condition, walk-in closets throughout.

Address:	210 Rose Ave.		
Date listed/Offering price:	11/01/98	$ 162,500	
Date sold/Sales price:	12/15/98	$ 158,900	
BRs/BA/Square feet:	3 BR	1.75 BA	1,765 SF

Comments: Nice home, good condition, large family room but small BRs.

Homes Currently For Sale: Flowerwood Area

CMA prepared by: John Bigbucks, Bigbucks Real Estate Co.
Date prepared: 02/05/99

Address: 147 Rose Ave.

Date listed/Offering price: 12/15/98 $ 169,990

BRs/BA/Square feet: 3 BR   2 BA   1,695 SF

Comments: Good shape, remodeled master bath, year-old roof.

Address: 289 Rose Ave.

Date listed/Offering Price: 12/08/98 $ 168,000

BRs/BA/Square feet: 3 BR   1.75 BA   1,640 SF

Comments: OK shape, nice yard and fruit trees.

Address: 140 Lilly Dr.

Date listed/Offering price: 11/28/98 $ 169,000

BRs/BA/Square feet: 3 BR   2 BA   1,680 SF

Comments: Good shape, upgraded plumbing, carport instead of garage.

Address: 196 Poppy St.

Date listed/Offering price: 11/01/98 $ 193,000

BRs/BA/Square feet: 4 BR   2 BA   1,750 SF

Comments: Fair shape, has extra bedroom but no built-in appliances.

If the CMA you obtain shows that prices for comps have been falling, forget about buying in the community unless at least two different agents you contact can provide a reasonable explanation for the declining values.

Also note that all the properties in the for sale section of the sample CMA are listed for at least a few thousand dollars more than similar homes that recently sold. The sellers will probably have to reduce their asking price a bit when they begin negotiating with buyers. But even after the negotiations are concluded and the sales close, prices in the neighborhood will be even higher than they were several months ago. It's another sign that prices are on an upward trend, so the neighborhood might be a good place to buy.

Price per Square Foot

Another way to analyze the results of a CMA is to look at properties based on what they're selling (or have sold) for on a square-foot basis. It's an easy calculation: Simply divide each home's asking or sales price by the the home's number of square feet.

For example, take a look at the information concerning the two homes on Rose Avenue and the house on Lilly Drive in the for sale section of the sample CMA. If you take each home's offering price and divide it by its square feet, you'll see that the asking price for all three homes is in the $100-per-square-foot range. Perform that same analysis on the Poppy Street house, which is only a block away, and you'll find that its offering price works out to a much higher $115-a-foot average.

The Poppy Street property has an extra bedroom but that doesn't explain why its per-square-foot average is so much higher than those of other homes in the neighborhood. Maybe the higher average is warranted because Poppy is a quieter street than Rose or Lilly, or because the house has special features that aren't mentioned in the CMA. More than likely, however, the seller on Poppy is simply asking for far more than the house is really worth. The only way to be sure is to personally visit all the homes that are listed on your CMA.

Spotting CMA Flaws

Just as a good CMA can provide vital clues about a neighborhood's price trends, a poorly prepared or incomplete report can be extremely misleading. Here are some key points to keep in mind while you review a CMA:

- *Make sure the homes listed are truly comparable.* If you're looking for a three-bedroom house, price information about homes that are much larger or smaller isn't terribly useful even if those homes are located right down the street. The CMA should also include remarks about each property's condition because a home that's in good shape is obviously worth more than a similar-size home that's falling apart. A good CMA helps you compare apples to apples, not apples to oranges.

- *Be wary of outdated comps.* Price information, like a loaf of bread, grows stale and eventually becomes useless as time passes. You can usually ignore any price data that appears on your CMA if it concerns a transaction that closed more than a year ago because it's too old to provide any insight on what's been going on recently. If sales in the neighborhood have been unusually strong, data that's more than six or even as few as three months old can be rendered useless.

- *Personally view every comp that you can.* A good CMA provides valuable insight about general price trends but you must supplement the research by visiting as many of those properties as you possibly can. Eyeballing each home, both inside and out, is the only way to determine whether the homes that appear on the CMA are really comparable. The more homes you visit, the better you'll get at determining which properties are overpriced, which ones are fairly priced, and which ones represent the best bargains.

Grading Local Schools

We talked a little bit about the importance of buying in an area that's served by good local schools in chapter 2. The quality of the schools that serve the neighborhood is important, even if you don't have school-age children yourself. Buyers are almost always willing to pay extra for a home in an area with good schools, and studies have consistently shown that home values in those areas nearly always rise faster than prices in communities where schools are below average. In short, buying in an area where schools are good will vastly improve your chances of making even bigger profits when you eventually sell.

If you're working with a real estate agent, the agent can tell you which schools serve the local neighborhood. If you aren't using an agent, the names of the local kindergarten, elementary, and high school that serves the area should be printed on the little For Sale flyer that's handed to you when you visit a seller's open house.

Agents and sellers realize that most buyers are particularly interested in the quality of the schools that serve their area, so they're prone to exaggeration. You can't afford to take their statements as gospel, just as you can't afford to put much stock in their comments about recent price trends. The only way to get a realistic picture of the local school system is to check how the schools have fared against schools in neighboring areas, and then supplement your research by touring the schools yourself.

Getting Test Results

If you're lucky, you can find out how the schools that serve a particular neighborhood have performed against other schools in surrounding areas simply by contacting each school's principal's office. But not all school administrators are willing to share such information, especially if their students have performed badly on state-administered tests. If you can't get the information you need from the school itself, try the district's headquarters. If you strike out there, call the state's education department and ask for help. Many libraries keep test score comparisons for schools in their area, and newspapers often publish special reports when test scores are released.

An even better idea is to order a report from one of the many independent, private sector companies that specialize in compiling information about different schools.

You can usually find the names of companies that operate in your targeted neighborhoods by checking the yellow pages of the phone book, under the headings of "School Information Services" or "Educational Resources." Prices vary, but usually range between $10 and $30 per report.

Now, here's a terrific bargain: Starting in 1998, a company called the International Real Estate Directory hooked up with the respected National School Reporting Services Inc. to offer buyers a free report aimed at helping them find a school that best fits their needs. The comprehensive report can compare up to six districts and includes lots of vital statistics concerning test scores, teacher-student ratios, and the like. The catch is that you have to use the Internet to take advantage of this free offer, which means you'll have to get a friend with Net access to order the report if you can't get on the Internet yourself. To request this very useful report, go to http://www.ired.com/market/schoolreport.htm.

Regardless of how you get the statistical information about local schools, it's important to actually visit the facilities themselves. A clean and quiet school with lots of well-kept students can tell you a lot about a facility than even the most comprehensive written report cannot. Similarly, a facility with graffiti-scarred walls and lots of tough-looking students milling about says reams about both the school and the surrounding neighborhood.

VISIT THE WEB

The Web site operated by the International Real Estate Directory (http://www.ired.com) is loaded with statistics and other useful information for first-time buyers. It also features a powerful search function and fast links to literally hundreds of other good sites.

Collaring Crime Stats

The level of a neighborhood's crime rate can have as great an impact on a home's resale value as the quality of its schools. In some cases, crime can play an even greater role than education in determining whether a neighborhood's property values will rise or fall. And obviously, you wouldn't enjoy living in an area if you were afraid to go out at night or were tempted to put on a bulletproof vest before going out to pick up the morning newspaper.

The process of choosing a neighborhood with a low crime rate is similar to the process involved in finding an area that features good schools. Again, you can't automatically trust what a sales agent or a seller says; you need to get the cold statistics yourself. And after you've checked out the stats, you'll need to walk around the neighborhood to determine how safe you'd really feel if you lived there.

Getting the Numbers

Crime-related statistics are available from several sources. The most comprehensive figures are published by the Federal Bureau of Investigation, whose periodic reports are kept in the reference areas of many major libraries. You can also access the FBI's information online (http://www.fbi.gov) but you will first have to download the software program Adobe Acrobat Reader if your computer doesn't already have the program installed. The download is free but can tie up your computer for more than an hour if you have an older machine.

One problem with using the FBI's stats is that they don't give you many tools to make meaningful comparisons between one neighborhood and another. A better way to get crime-related information is to order a report from the growing number of private-sector companies that not only gather data but then analyze them to issue what amounts to a letter grade (A, B+, C–, and so forth) for different areas. These companies can usually be found in the yellow pages of the phone book, under the "Security" or even "Real Estate Services" headings. Each report typically costs $20, so you should obviously use your discretion when ordering. One of the better companies that offer online crime-related reports is CrimeCheck (http://www.crimecheck.com), which charges $20 and can usually send the report to your computer within a few hours.

VISIT THE WEB

Two Internet sites (http://www.realtor.com and http://www.homeadvisor.com) include free crime-related statistics and other information about several hundred neighborhoods across the country. Go to each site and use their search function, keyword: crime.

Supplementing Your Search

Regardless of how you obtain crime stats for the neighborhoods you're checking out, it's equally important to visit the local police department and talk to the desk sergeant or community relations officer. They can provide more information about crime trends in the neighborhood and can often provide insight that you can't get by reading cold statistical reports. For example, the stats might indicate that a seemingly fine neighborhood has a serious crime problem. By talking to the desk sergeant, you might discover that the problems are limited to only one or two streets or that most of the crime stems from a particular building or shopping center. It would probably be OK to buy a house in such a neighborhood as long as you made sure your new home was a safe distance away from the troublesome street or project.

Here are some other tips to help you find the safest areas:

- *Visit each neighborhood at least three or four times,* both during the day and at night. Also make sure you visit both during the week and on weekends. Some neighborhoods are like Dr. Jekyll and Mr. Hyde: They're perfectly charming on weekdays but downright dangerous after sundown or on the weekend.

- *Read the local newspapers.* Many newspapers publish crime blotters, listing recent crimes and where they occurred. You obviously want to avoid areas, streets, or neighborhoods that are frequently mentioned in the blotter.

- *Check for houses with security bars on the windows.* If nearly every house in the area has bars on the windows or protective steel doors instead of screens, it's a sign that people who already live there (and know a lot more than you do) are worried about their safety.

- *Look for graffiti and other telltale signs of trouble.* Graffiti is often a sign that crime in the area is already a problem, or will become a problem soon. Other warning signs include loiterers, suspicious looking cars, and local stores that have a security guard posted at their doorway or more surveillance equipment than the Pentagon.

Assessing Amenities

The three most important things to remember when choosing a neighborhood is to focus on areas where prices are rising, schools are good, and crime is firmly under control. Here are some other features you might want to look for, although they're not nearly as important as the first three:

- *Lots of parks.* This can be particularly important if you have kids or if you don't like dodging cars when you take your morning jog.

- *Close to public transportation.* This is especially vital if you depend on buses, trains, or other types of public transit to get around.

- *Nearby shopping.* You certainly want to be fairly close to a supermarket, and maybe even a large shopping complex if you're a mall rat.

- *Cultural facilities.* You might want to be close to museums, playhouses, or the like if that's the kind of stuff that interests you.

- *Entertainment options.* Having to drive crosstown to catch a movie or visit a decent restaurant is a drag.

- *Places of worship.* Attend a couple of services at local churches or synagogues to see how you like the congregation and its leaders.

Checkin' Out the House

Choosing the home you want to buy is a lot like finding the person you'd like to marry: Everyone you know has an opinion about your choice, but you're the one who gets to make the final selection. And, like choosing a husband or wife, your decision about which home to purchase is probably going to be influenced by a variety of factors that only you can explain—particularly that special gut feeling you get after you've checked out all the other candidates and know that this is the one I really, really want. Warts and all.

OK, we'll admit that this "buying-a-home-is-like-choosing-a-spouse" analogy doesn't quite work. But you get the picture.

At this point, most other real estate authors would present a long string of cliché pearls of wisdom that even the greenest first-time buyer already knows. We'll give you a little more credit than that, figuring that we don't need to waste page after precious page (and several minutes of your time) to remind you how important it is to choose a home that has indoor plumbing.

You just learned how to choose the best and most affordable neighborhoods, so you obviously should limit your search to those one or two areas that meet the criteria we laid down a few pages earlier. Hopefully, you have followed the advice in chapter 1 by getting preapproved for a loan. If so, you know how much you can spend on a house and you won't waste time looking at properties that you can't afford. Also, you should have filled out the "wants versus needs" checklist from chapter 2, which will help focus your search for the perfect home. Now you need to visit the properties that fit within all the parameters. Follow these additional pointers to narrow your list of prospective candidates down to no more than two or three homes:

- *Keep referring to your comparative market analysis.* The CMA will help you determine whether or not each home you visit is reasonably priced, at least when compared to other properties that are available in the same neighborhood. Also bring along a copy of your completed "wants versus needs" checklist when you visit each open house. Doing so will help you avoid paying extra for features you don't really need.

- *Pay attention to each property's "floor plan functionality."* You might find several homes that include all the features listed on your "wants versus needs" checklist. The next step is to envision what it would be like to live in the house and decide if its floor plan makes sense. Are the bathrooms situated in logical places or would guests have to traipse through a bedroom before finding a toilet? Is the kitchen designed intelligently or is the sink on one side of the room and the dishwasher on the other? Homes that have been expanded once or twice over the years are especially notorious for having floor plans that Archie Bunker might call "dingier than a dingbat."

- *Approach "fixer uppers" carefully.* Homes that merely need inexpensive cosmetic repairs—such as a fresh coat of paint, better landscaping, and new carpet—are often great bargains because the relatively small investment needed to make the improvements can add thousands of dollars to the property's resale value. Conversely, homes that need major repairs can turn into the proverbial "money pit": Buying a home that's listed for $10,000 less than all the other properties in the neighborhood is a losing proposition if it needs $20,000 in repairs.

- *Try to get a feel for each seller's motivation level.* The more anxious the seller, the better chance you have of getting a great deal. A vacant home is often a sign that the owners are ready and willing to bargain, perhaps because they have already bought another house and they are now saddled with two monthly mortgage payments instead of one. Your agent may also be privy to important information about the seller's motivation: Homeowners who are divorcing or whose employers are transferring them out of town are typically among those who are the most eager to deal.

- *Think about your future housing needs.* Studies show that first-time buyers typically stay in their home for five years, so keep that in mind as you view the properties that are for sale. You might need to focus your search on homes that have an extra bedroom or convertible den if you're single but expect to get married soon or if you're already married and are planning to have a child or two in the next few years. But you might be able to settle for a house that's smaller and less expensive if, say, you have a teenage kid that's about to leave for college.

The Five Fatal Flaws

As you'll see in the next chapter, any offer you make on a house you want to buy should be contingent on the home passing the examination of a professional inspector. But you can't afford to have an inspector look at every property you visit because each inspection can cost $200 or more. To save time and avoid unnecessary inspection fees, if a home you tour has one or more of the five costly problems discussed below it's usually best to scratch it from your list of potential candidates.

• *Outdated or faulty wiring.* Older homes are especially susceptible to this common problem but some newer homes suffer from it, too. Outdated wiring can make it impossible to run a dishwasher or other modern appliance without first making costly upgrades. Faulty wiring presents safety hazards and can be equally costly to repair. Exposed wiring, lots of extension cords, a fuse box that has old-fashioned glass fuses instead of switches, or a lack of new appliances are often signs of serious electrical deficiencies.

• *Bad plumbing.* A leaky faucet is easy and inexpensive to fix. But toilets that are slow to flush, drains that take forever to clear, and standing water in a sink are often indicators that far more serious (and costly) plumbing repairs are needed.

• *Defective roof.* Missing, loose, peeling, or flaking shingles are signs that the roof needs major repairs or might need to be entirely replaced. Another sign of roofing problems is stains you notice on the ceiling as you tour the rooms inside the house. It can easily cost $3,000 to replace the roof on a typical 1,500-square-foot home, and much more if top quality material is used or the roof itself has complicated angles or curves.

- *Foundation problems.* A slipping or seriously cracked foundation can be very expensive to repair or replace. A noticeable slanting of the floors or several doors and windows that won't open and shut properly are often signs that the home's foundation needs work. Standing water around the rim of the house also can (but not always) indicate problems with the foundation or that the property has drainage problems that could be costly to remedy.

- *Termites or other pests.* Pest-related damage isn't always easy to spot, which is why any offer you eventually make will probably involve examinations by at least two inspectors—a generalist and a second inspector who'll hunt for problems caused by termites, beetles, fungus, or similar pests that are common in the area. But if you can spot extensive infestations or other major problems with your naked eye, you can probably scratch the home off your list immediately. There's almost certain to be even worse trouble lurking under the floor, inside the walls, or up near the roof.

How many homes should you visit before you decide on the one or two that you're actually willing to pursue? You must certainly tour at least ten to get a rough idea of what's available and an inkling about which homes represent the best bargains. Visiting 20 or 30 properties would be even better. But if you visit more than 40 or 50 homes without finding at least one that you think merits an offer, you might need to lower your expectations a bit. Take another look at the "wants versus needs" checklist you completed earlier to see if one or more of the features you originally checked as being "must have" can be shifted over to the "would like to have" column.

No matter how many houses you visit, the fact that you're now reaching the middle of this book means that you're well on your way to buying your first home. Congratulations, and keep reading!

Top Five Things to Do Right Now

1. Set your own pace. It takes time to find the best neighborhood you can afford and the two or three homes that are the best deals. Don't let an aggressive agent or seller push you into making an offer before you're ready.

2. Get a CMA for each neighborhood that interests you. A good comparable market analysis can tell you whether prices in the area are rising or falling. Never buy in a neighborhood where prices are dropping because values will likely skid even further in the months or years ahead.

3. Check out the schools and local crime stats. Homes cost more in neighborhoods that have good public schools and a low crime rate but it's impossible to put a price tag on the quality of a kid's education or your personal sense of security. Besides, values in "good" areas almost always rise faster than prices in communities with subpar schools and high levels of crime.

4. Zero in on the one or two best deals in the best neighborhood you can afford. Your CMA will prove handy again because it should list all the properties that are for sale in the area and the prices that other buyers have recently paid for comparable homes.

5. Get ready to make an offer. If you haven't taken the time to get preapproved for a mortgage, do it now. Your ability to get the seller to accept a lower sales price or make other valuable concessions will be enhanced if a lender has already agreed to provide you the financing needed to quickly close the transaction.

MAKING *the* **Right** *Offer*

CHAPTER FIVE

No one wants to pay too much for a home or to buy a house and discover hidden problems later. Taking a few simple steps now will help to ensure that you don't overpay and also limit the chance that you'll have problems after the sale closes.

Buying a home involves all sorts of paperwork. But of all those documents and forms, the most important will be the purchase offer you prepare when you first offer to buy the home. The purchase offer must include all sorts of details, from big ticket items such as the price you're willing to pay to the minutiae of whether the transaction includes the old rug in the hall.

A well-written offer will prevent you from paying too much for the home, sharply reduce the chances that something will go wrong after the contract is signed, and protect you if an insolvable problem eventually develops. A poorly constructed offer is an invitation to a disaster party, with you as the host who must pay the bill.

Setting a Price

The first step toward making a winning offer is to determine the maximum amount that you're willing to pay for the home. The initial price you offer to pay will probably be less than what you think the home is really worth. For obvious reasons, making your best offer first will destroy your power to negotiate a better deal. But knowing in advance how high you're willing to go will shape your strategy as you bargain with the seller—or tell you when to walk away from the bargaining table and look for a different home if the seller's demands are unreasonable.

Establishing the home's actual market value isn't really that difficult, as long as you've got the type of thorough comparative market analysis we discussed in the previous chapter and you have visited all the properties on the CMA yourself to make sure the properties are truly comparable. Making an offer on a home without first obtaining a comprehensive CMA is tantamount to marching into battle by yourself, armed with nothing but a toothpick. Having a good CMA is like having Rambo by your side and a bazooka on your shoulder.

While a thorough CMA will help you establish how much the property is worth on the open market, only you can decide how much you're willing to pay for the home. Your market analysis might indicate a home is worth $140,000 but you may decide that you won't pay a nickel over $130,000 because the home doesn't quite fit your needs or you haven't been preapproved for a loan that's large enough to pay the higher price. Or you might be willing to pay a little more than the price your CMA indicates the property is worth if values in the area are rising fast or if the seller is willing to pay most of the closing costs or make other valuable concessions.

Writing the Offer

All prospective real estate deals must first be put in writing. This includes your initial offer, the seller's counteroffer, and the agreement you finally reach after negotiations are concluded. An agreement that's sealed with a mere handshake or a promise that isn't put down on paper is worthless and almost always unenforceable in court. As movie mogul Sam Goldwyn once said, "A verbal agreement isn't worth the paper it's written on."

If you're working with a real estate agent, the agent will have all the preprinted forms you need to make an offer and respond to the seller's counteroffer. You can purchase standard fill-in-the-blanks forms from most business supply or stationery stores if you're handling the offer yourself but it would be better to ask an agent you know for a copy of the forms he or she uses. The forms agents use are usually written by top real estate attorneys and are regularly updated to reflect changes in the law. Some store-bought forms are virtually worthless because they were created years ago, when buying a home wasn't nearly as complicated as it is today.

VISIT THE WEB

Microsoft's outstanding Internet real estate Web site includes a step-by-step guide to help you prepare a winning offer. Go to http://www.homeadvisor.com and click the "Offer and Closing" heading.

Regardless of how you obtain your form, it's important to review it before you sit down and start filling in the blanks. Knowing all the components of a typical offer will help you begin structuring the deal in your mind before you start writing it down on paper, which in turn will help move the process along faster.

Your Initial Offering Price

Though your CMA will give you a good idea about how much the home is worth, your initial offer is probably going to be lower. But should it be 5 percent less than the home's apparent value? Maybe 10 percent? Perhaps even 20 or 30 percent?

Alas, there's no rule of thumb here for you to follow. If sales in the area are fairly steady and the number of buyers roughly matches the number of sellers, your first offer probably should be between 5 and 10 percent below the price you believe the home is actually worth. If sales in the area are slowing, the home is vacant, or you have reasons to believe the seller is unusually anxious to make a deal, you might be able to offer 10 or even 20 percent below its market value.

Conversely, your initial offer will probably have to be at or near the property's market value if sales are strong or the home appears to be a terrific bargain. It would be

both foolish and heartbreaking to lose a great deal just because you wanted to save an additional $1,000 or $2,000.

Should You Lowball?

Some self-proclaimed real estate experts say your first offer should automatically be at least 20 or 30 percent below the market value suggested by your CMA. "You can always negotiate your offer upward," they say. But the truth is, the only time such a lowball offer is justified is when your CMA shows that the house you want is way overpriced or you have reason to believe that the seller is extremely anxious to unload the property. Otherwise, the seller is going to immediately reject your offer and—even worse—probably assume that you're not really serious about purchasing the home. Even if you follow up your lowball offer with a more realistic one, the seller might be insulted enough to refuse to deal with you even if you were the last buyer on earth. Lowball offers are almost always a waste of time for both the buyer who makes them and the seller who fields them. Your initial offering price doesn't have to be for full price but it should at least be in the ballpark of what the seller can reasonably expect to receive.

Details, Details

Determining your initial offering price is important but it's only one component of a well-written purchase offer that will grab the seller's attention while also protecting your interests. Here are some other issues that your offer must address:

- *Financing the transaction.* The way you plan to finance your purchase can have a huge impact on the seller's willingness to negotiate and the chances that you'll eventually reach an agreement. For example, most sellers tend to favor offers from buyers who are willing to make a large down payment because a large down payment reduces the amount of money the buyer must borrow, improving the chance that a bank will make the loan. Conversely, many sellers frown on offers from buyers who plan to make a small down payment (or none at all) because this creates a greater possibility that a lender won't provide the financing. You'll

learn about an important contingency involving financing later in this chapter.

- *Size of your deposit.* When you make an offer, you're expected to include a deposit to show that you're serious about closing the deal. There's no set rule that determines how large your deposit should be but most range from 1 percent to 5 percent of the purchase price. The check you write will probably be deposited in a special account that's held by the seller's broker or it will be passed along to the escrow agent or closing attorney who will supervise all the paperwork involved in completing the transaction. The deposit must be returned to you if the sale falls apart through no fault of your own. But if you decide to cancel simply because you get cold feet or find a different house to buy, the seller can usually keep the money as compensation for the seller's wasted time.

- *Items included in the sale.* It's safe to assume that certain components of the home—such as the roof, underground pipes, and the driveway—will be included in your purchase. It's not exaggerating much to say that everything else is pretty much negotiable. The list on page 74 details some of the most common items that buyers often expect to be included in a sale but sellers typically think they can take with them when they move. Any item you want to be part of the transaction should be incorporated in the main body of your purchase offer or included in an addendum.

- *Closing date.* It will probably take at least 30 to 45 days for an appraisal to be made, inspections performed, and all the sale-related paperwork to be processed. It's not unusual for the process to take 60 days, especially if the market is hot and appraisers, inspectors, and all the other professionals involved in the sale are backlogged. You might need to give yourself even more time if, say, leaving your apartment earlier would result in a huge financial penalty or there's another good reason that prevents you from moving quickly. The sellers will also have a time schedule, so pick a reasonable closing date based on your own requirements and assume that you'll have to negotiate a compromise later.

Yours, Mine, or Whose?

As a general rule, the offer you make to buy a home automatically includes anything that's "fixed" to the house. This sounds simple enough, but laws in most states don't clearly define which items are fixtures that the buyer can expect to keep and which ones are personal possessions that the seller can take when the deal closes. Review the list of items below and, if you want to include any of them in your transaction, make sure your offer specifically states you'll have the right to keep them when the deal closes.

- Appliances, especially if they aren't built-in or affixed to a cabinet or pantry

- Bookshelves

- Air-conditioning and heating units (portable units are a common source of disputes, even if they're installed in a window or sit on a shelf)

- Drapes, curtains, and other window coverings

- Rugs and similar floor coverings, especially those that could be easily removed

- Ceiling fans

- Wall coverings, pictures, and other artwork

- Fireplace, pool, or spa equipment

- Sheds and similar outdoor structures

- Semiportable fences and gates, especially if they have wheels on the bottom

- *Division of closing costs.* Local custom typically dictates which closing costs the buyer pays for and which costs are paid by the seller. But in the end, virtually every type of closing cost is negotiable. The seller might agree to pay most or all of the costs if sales in the area are slow or if the owner is anxious to close a deal because he or she has already bought another home. But you might have to pay most or all of the costs if homes in the area are selling like hotcakes or you're sure the seller is pondering offers from other buyers.

Again, if you're working with a real estate agent, the agent's knowledge and expertise will prove invaluable as you write your offer. If you're not using an agent, you'd be wise to hire one on an hourly or flat-fee basis to help you complete the offer and assist in any negotiations. Many real estate lawyers and escrow officers also offer their services for a flat fee or hourly rate.

Building an Escape Hatch

Regardless of how badly you want to purchase a particular property, it's imperative that you have at least a couple of escape hatches to crawl through that will cancel the sale if something goes wrong after your offer has been accepted. In real estate parlance, such escape hatches are called *contingencies*. There are two key contingencies that you absolutely must include in any offer you make: financing and inspection.

Financing Contingency

The first key contingency you must include is called a *financing contingency*. It lets you cancel the sale and get your deposit back if you can't get a suitable mortgage.

We'll assume that you followed the advice in chapter 2 by getting preapproved for a mortgage. Even though preapproval greatly enhances your chances of getting the financing you'll need to close the deal, the lender can still revoke its approval for any number of reasons. Here are a few:

- *Your financial situation or credit rating has taken a turn for the worse.* The lender can cancel its earlier loan approval if, say, your income has recent-

ly dropped, your debt load has increased, or a new black mark has appeared on your credit record. It can even be revoked if you've changed jobs and received a raise.

- *Interest rates have jumped since the preapproval was granted.* First-time buyers are especially susceptible to interest rate swings, because they often have a hard time qualifying for a mortgage even when rates are low. A lender can cancel a preapproval if rates have since risen to the point where you no longer qualify for a loan.

- *The lender's appraiser determines you're paying too much for the home.* No bank issues a mortgage without first having an appraiser determine the property's market value. Say you have agreed to pay $125,000 for the home but the appraiser decides it's worth only $115,000. The lender is under no obligation to finance the purchase, even if you've got the ability to add an extra $10,000 to your down payment and the bank recently preapproved you for a $1 million mortgage.

The main lesson here is that lenders can reject your loan application or revoke an earlier loan approval for any number of reasons. If you have included a standard loan contingency in your purchase offer, you can cancel the sale and get your deposit back. But if you failed to include the contingency, the seller has the right to keep your deposit and put the home back on the market.

Inspection Contingency

The second contingency every offer should include concerns the home's overall quality. This *inspection contingency* will let you cancel the transaction and get your deposit back if a professional inspection uncovers problems but the seller refuses to make needed repairs.

Roughly 80 percent of all homebuyers—and 100 percent of the smart ones—make their purchase offer contingent upon the property passing the examination of a professional inspector. It's the best way to find out if the home is structurally sound or, instead, has hidden defects that could be costly to repair. Can that leaky faucet be

Sample Contingencies

Most preprinted purchase offers include the two most important contingencies: one that protects you in case you can't get financing for the deal and another that lets you bail out without penalty if the home fails a professional inspection. But if the form you use doesn't include these two vital elements, the sample contingencies below can be used as a basis to write your own clauses with the help of a skilled real estate agent or attorney.

Basic Financing Contingency

"This offer is contingent upon Buyer obtaining satisfactory financing secured by said property. Buyer shall have the sole and exclusive right to determine whether the financing available is deemed satisfactory. If Buyer is unable to obtain such financing within 30 days of this offer, Buyer must notify Seller in writing of Buyer's election to cancel this contract and have Buyer's deposit returned in a reasonable amount of time."

Basic Inspection Contingency

"This offer is contingent upon a professional inspection of said property. Buyer shall have the sole and exclusive right to select the inspector and must pay for said inspector's services. Buyer shall also have the sole and exclusive right to determine whether the results of said inspection are deemed satisfactory. If Buyer determines results of said inspection are not satisfactory within 10 days after the completed inspection results are received by Buyer, Buyer must notify Seller in writing of Buyer's election to cancel this contract and have Buyer's deposit returned in a reasonable amount of time."

fixed with a five-cent washer or is it a sign that the home's entire plumbing system is shot and needs $4,500 in repairs? Do those windows that won't close all the way simply need a squirt of household oil or are they evidence that the foundation is slipping and must be replaced to the tune of $25,000? Only a professional inspector is qualified to answer those questions for you.

Including a standard inspection contingency in your purchase offer will protect you in a couple of ways. If the inspection turns up problems, you can demand that the seller either pay for the repairs, lower the agreed-upon sales price, or make other concessions to offset the cost of making the repairs yourself. Should the seller refuse to renegotiate terms of the deal, the inspection contingency will allow you to cancel the sale and get your deposit back. But if you're foolish enough to omit the inspection contingency from your offer, the seller will have no obligation to make any needed repairs and can keep your deposit if you decide to back out of your offer because the home has so many problems.

Other Contingencies

It's imperative to include both a financing and inspection contingency in your purchase offer. They've become so commonplace that sellers rarely object to their presence.

Technically, you can include as many contingencies as you want in your purchase offer. The important thing to remember is that the more contingencies you include, the less attractive your offer becomes. Each contingency attaches one more string to your proposal, and sellers don't like offers that come with too many strings attached. Nevertheless, here are some other contingencies you may want to include in addition to the ones that cover financing and a home inspection.

- *Association contingency.* If the home is in a development that's ruled by a homeowners association or similar group, your offer should include a contingency that allows you or your accountant to inspect the organization's financial records to determine its soundness and that gives you the right to review its bylaws and related documents to decide if you can live within the association's rules.

- *Title contingency.* This contingency allows you to cancel the sale and get your deposit back if you cannot obtain a title insurance policy on the home because there are questions involving the home's ownership records.

- *Permit contingency.* Adding this contingency to your purchase offer typically makes your offer contingent on the seller's ability to produce evidence that the home meets local building requirements and that any additions or remodeling jobs have been approved by the appropriate government authorities.

- *Variance or zoning contingency.* This contingency often involves either the way the current owner uses the property or how you plan to use it. For example, if you're buying in a neighborhood where no businesses are allowed but hope to use the home's extra bedroom as an office, you may want to make your offer contingent on your ability to get your plan approved by local zoning officials. If you can't get the plan approved, you can cancel the transaction and get your deposit back.

Top Five Things to Do Right Now

1. Get a copy of a standard purchase offer contract. Familiarize yourself with its contents so you can structure your proposal in your mind before you start writing it down on paper.

2. Review your comparative market analysis. The CMA is the best way to determine how much a home is really worth but it may need to be updated if it's more than a month or two old.

3. Find a professional to help write your offer. If you aren't using an agent, get help from a veteran real estate attorney, title company, or full-time escrow officer to complete all the paperwork and shepherd the deal to a successful close.

4. Understand how contingencies work. Any offer you make should include contingencies involving financing and an inspection and you may feel safer adding additional ones.

5. Get ready to negotiate. Virtually all transactions involve some level of negotiation, which is what the next chapter is all about.

Negotiating *to* Win-Win

Long, long ago, in a far-off and magic land, a handsome and happy couple placed their castle, which had become too small for them, on the market. Minutes after hammering a For Sale sign into the front lawn, they spotted a beautiful, long-haired woman galloping up on their driveway on a white horse.

"This," she pronounced grandly, "is my new home."

"Madam, we do ask $120,000," the handsome, happy couple said.

"I offer thee $118,000," responded the stranger.

"We shall take this, thy first offer," said the couple. "In other words, it's a deal."

The beautiful stranger moved into her new home. The couple took up residence in their new, bigger castle. And they all lived . . . well, you know the rest.

This is a sweet fairy tale, but a fairy tale is all it is. Unless you match a list price exactly, very, very few sellers will accept a first offer. In fact, five or six counteroffers between you and the seller should not be viewed as uncommon.

Negotiation ABCs

Between your first offer and the close lies the homebuying chore that most new buyers dread most: negotiation. You may not think of yourself as the world's greatest bargainer. Other than when scoping out garage sales, you may have never haggled over price before. And getting someone to drop 25 cents off the cost of some slightly used books is a lot easier than getting homesellers to drop several grand off the price of their palace.

Have no fear. Your confusion will ebb once you've learned some negotiating strategies. The techniques discussed later in this chapter will help. But first things first. Let's start off by taking a look at the major steps in homebuying negotiations.

1. You make an offer, which the seller either accepts outright, rejects outright or, most commonly, presents a counteroffer.

2. You review the seller's offer, accept it, reject it, or write up a counteroffer.

3. The process continues in this vein until you reach a deal or until one party decides to walk away from the table.

Before learning the techniques that will help you negotiate a sales price that proves acceptable to both parties, you need to keep a few precepts in mind.

Adopt a Win-Win Attitude

You begin your home hunting knowing that, in all probability, you and the seller will have to negotiate over the terms of purchase. What type of attitude toward negotiations should you embrace? Many successful homebuyers have found negotiations more palatable when they adopt a "win-win attitude." The mind-set goes like this: You want to get a good deal on a property you like and you want the seller to walk away satisfied with your overall offer. You win; the seller wins.

This attitude, once espoused, will begin to permeate all your interactions with your agent and the seller. It will make you more reasonable, help keep your emotions in check, and make negotiations easier.

Sellers Get Emotional; You Keep Your Head

Sellers are a temperamental lot. They think of their houses as extensions of themselves. All the memories imbued in the place make it seem special to them. And it is. But sometimes their pride of ownership will lead them to ask for an unreasonable purchase price. They may get ticked off at any suggestion that their house is worth anything less than comparable houses in the area, plus an additional 10 percent for their memories.

As a first-time buyer, you carry no such emotional baggage. No matter how much you may love the structure of the house you hope to buy, you have no emotional attachment. Until you move in, cuddle with your loved ones, fight with your loved ones, get a new puppy, light the fireplace, it ain't a home. It's just a house.

Sellers get emotional. You keep your head, stay reasonable, and bend when appropriate. Keep your eye on the prize: a house you want, at a good price.

Remember Who You're Talking To

In chapter 3 you learned about the difference between buyer's agents and seller's agents. Now it's time to take that information to heart. If you have chosen to work with a seller's agent, be very, very careful of what you reveal in the agent's presence. Remember, the agent's loyalties lie with the seller. If you start making pronouncements along the lines of, "Well, we're offering $125,000, but we're willing to go to $130,000," or "God, I don't have much time until my company relocates. I just have to have this place," the agent, by law, must report the information back to the seller. The point is this: When working with a seller's agent, watch your mouth—it could cost you.

If you've chosen to work with a buyer's agent, you can be much more up front about your desires and negotiating plans. Remember, the loyalty of a buyer's broker goes to you. A buyer's agent can therefore fill you in on information gleaned about the sellers—their motivation for listing their home, the minimum offer they will take, and so forth. Again, a seller's broker works for the current homeowner and would be unable to divulge this type of information.

Knowledge Is Power

The stronger the seller's market, the nearer you will have to come to the list price to win the home you want. Still, even in the tightest markets you can find people who are termed, in real estate lingo, "motivated sellers." Who are they?

Motivated sellers are people who, for whatever reason, have to—or really, really want to—get out of their current digs. They include:

- People who have to move due to job relocations

- Divorcing couples

- Empty nesters, or people whose children have grown and now want to move to smaller quarters

- People who have inherited houses. Say great aunt Harriet left to her favorite nephew, Bob, her two-bedroom condo in Tampa. Bob lives in New York. All he wants to do is sell the place, get his cash, and get on with his life.

- People who have had the house on the market for a long time. These folks are probably itching to move by now.

Talk to your real estate agent about the seller's motivation for moving. A buyer's broker should tell you everything he or she knows. A seller's broker will probably prove less open but may still let a few nuggets drop.

Don't think for a minute that you're the only negotiator trying to get a handle on the other party. The seller will undoubtedly scope you out, too. You may even meet. Work hard to make any conversation with the seller cordial and friendly. Let's face it, a seller who likes you may be more willing to give you a break, where possible. Such a seller will almost certainly be happier to accommodate your wishes to come back with a measuring tape, to let you stop by with your folks, or to answer the door when your home inspector knocks. Still, during any contact with the seller, you should not reveal too much about yourself or your situation. You don't want to tip your hand toward the folks on the other side of the negotiating table.

Some real estate agents are so concerned about buyers divulging too much information to sellers that they practically go into conniptions to keep the two sides apart. Other agents will allow buyer and seller to meet, in the hope that a developing rapport will ease negotiations.

If you do meet a seller, here are some rules of thumb to follow:

- *Be polite and friendly but not particularly open.* If a seller asks you why you want his or her house, or why you're moving, you should respond with a vague "Oh, Bob and I thought it was time for a change, and we like this section of town, so we're looking at several neighborhoods." Don't say, "We're from out of town, we have to move here in a month because Bob's being relocated, and this is the only house that meets our needs."

- *Don't criticize the house.* Critical comments will only lead to bad feelings between you and the seller.

- *Don't gush over the house.* If you appear to have fallen in love, you've given the seller the upper hand.

Remember this: You want the seller to like you but not to really know you.

You don't have to walk such a fine social/psychological line when learning about the neighborhood, but knowing the list prices of comparable homes in the area can prove important to your negotiating strategy. With the help of your agent, compile

a list of houses that are now for sale or that have recently sold. Your list should include prices and amenities offered. You can use this information to gently nudge the sellers into the realization that they may be asking a bit too much for their home. This process, called *loading,* is discussed later in this chapter.

Negotiate It All!

What can you negotiate? Everything! Price will almost certainly prove the premiere bargaining point. But don't neglect other aspects of the sale. Sometimes issues other than price can help close the gap between what the seller wants you to pay and what you can afford.

Still, it's the price you fret over. Remember this: Sellers generally list their houses a bit too high at first. They do this on purpose because they expect to haggle. They're allowing themselves a bit of padding. The more you know about the seller and the neighborhood, the more you're able to tailor a reasonable and fair offer.

How to Hold Title to Your Home and Why You Should Care

Before you close on your new home, you need to decide what type of title you want. Title is the formal legal document that represents proof of ownership. Stop yawning and pay attention.

Single people who are buying a house are usually stuck with individual ownership. However, groups (married couples can be considered a group) can hold title in ways that protect themselves and the property in cases of lawsuits, bankruptcy, and death.

If you are buying a home with one or more other people, you may want to consider joint tenancy with the right of survivorship, tenants in common, or tenancy by the entirety—an option available only to married couples.

- *Joint tenancy with the right of survivorship.* Allowing for two or more persons to own a home, this title makes transfer easy when one partner dies. Suppose Harry and Sue are married, and Harry dies. If the couple owns their home under a joint tenancy with right of survivorship title, ownership automatically passes to Sue when Harry dies.

- *Tenancy in common.* This type of title allows two or more people to buy a home with each member of the group owning a share in it. Shares need not be equal and members of the group can sell their shares at any time to anyone.

- *Tenancy by the entirety.* This title option, available to married couples only and not available in some states, protects the property against the debts incurred by either spouse. Say one spouse incurs a debt and fails to pay. The creditors will naturally hope to attach the house. However, the creditor cannot go after the house unless the other spouse—the one who has not incurred the debt—agrees. Because few spouses would ever sign off on such a plan, the creditor must wait to collect until the property is sold or the marriage is severed through divorce.

These are just some general title guidelines. Title forms, and protections offered, vary. Check with your real estate agent or an attorney to determine the best way for you to hold title to your new home.

The Nitty-Gritty

Sure, you would have loved the sellers to have accepted your first offer out of the box but, unfortunately, that rarely happens. In fact, a counteroffer is actually a good thing. It means that you didn't come in with such an insulting lowball bid that the seller rejected you out of hand. But now, here it sits—the counteroffer. It probably includes the fairly intimidating words "time is of the essence." This means that you only have until the time noted—usually a day or two—to proffer a new deal of your own.

Some of the seller's most common requests include asking the buyer to pay a higher price than originally offered; to pay all closing costs; and to push back the closing date. You have to decide what points you wish to negotiate. And before you say, "The price, stupid," consider this: Negotiating on items other than the selling price can help bridge the monetary gap separating you from the seller. Here are some examples:

- *Move in dates.* The seller can save hundreds or even thousands of dollars in temporary housing costs if you agree to push back the closing. Say you are offering a price $2,000 lower than the sellers demand and you ask to move in three weeks before the sellers' ideal closing date. Consider putting off the closing, thereby allowing the sellers to stay in their home for an extra three weeks. This will save the sellers the costs of temporary housing and they may be willing to deduct this amount from the selling price of the home.

- *Storage.* Will the sellers allow you to stash your stuff in their basement? Depending on when you have to vacate your apartment and when you can move into your new home, this may save you a chunk of change in storage fees. You can use this money toward the sales price.

- *Closing costs.* Ask the sellers if they can help you with closing costs in exchange for a higher price on the house. In certain very special cases— such as when dealing with an extremely motivated homeowner or an extraordinarily weak seller's market—you can ask the seller to pay all the closing fees. Be careful, however. Such a suggestion may annoy the seller and make further negotiations acrimonious. Your real estate agent can help you determine whether this is a reasonable request in your situation.

- *Refrigerators, washers, dryers, aboveground pools, spas, and so forth.* If the sellers are marketing their house with these amenities, see how they respond to keeping them in exchange for a lower price on the house. Ditto for homeowners offering furnished digs.

These are some common cases where savvy negotiations can help bring the buyer and seller closer to a price they can each live with. But you may also encounter some special circumstances demanding special consideration. These situations include dealing with the all-too-common 50–50 split; negotiating for an owner-financed home; a home inspector unearthing unexpected problems; and finding the deal of the millennium.

The 50-50 Split: Why It Works, and When It Doesn't

Your dream house lists for $95,000. You offer $90,000. The seller counteroffers—surprise!—$92,500. It seems fair and reasonable; in many cases it is. You and the owner agree to a sale price that sits midway between what the owner wants and what you initially offered.

But if you take some time to figure out why the seller demands that extra two-and-a-half-grand, you may be able to accommodate the seller's true needs without raising your offer.

For instance, would the owners be willing to come down to $90,000 if they didn't have to foot the bill for a month-long stay in a hotel because you hope to close a month before they can take possession of their new place? If you can postpone your closing date to a time that's more convenient to them, they may be willing to drop their price.

Or suppose the sellers recently bought a $2,000 aboveground pool, which, they have noted in their offer, "goes with the house." Because they have three kids who have grown accustomed to the joys of splashing around in the summer, they know they'll have to buy another one for their new home. Tell them to take the pool when they move, and see if they'll accept your $90,000 offer.

Often, a 50–50 split in the price differential is the fairest way to come to an offer that both buyer and seller can live with. However, if you can make other concessions that encourage the seller to come down to your offer, by all means do so.

Owner Financing

If you are buying an owner-financed home—a situation we'll discuss in detail in chapter 7—you can find several ways to renegotiate the deal so that the sellers get the price they want and you get a home you can afford. These include a lower cash deposit than originally requested and a lease-purchase plan with an extended close date.

If There Is Something Wrong with the House

The savvy consumer makes an offer contingent on a home inspection. But what do you do if the inspector unearths a surprise flaw—leaking pipes or an air conditioner gasping its last? You have several options. You can walk away from the contract, ask the owners to fix it, or renegotiate your price. Before making your decision, consider these issues:

- *Has the inspector found something that cannot be fixed?* Problems like polluted wells, the nearby presence of power lines and electromagnetic fields, or cracks in the foundation of the home usually cannot be rectified. If an inspection unearths these types of obstacles, you may need to walk away from the deal.

- *If a problem can be fixed, at what cost?* If a housing inspector has found a $10,000 problem with the electrical wiring in the home, are the sellers willing to pay for repair? If not, are they willing to drop the purchase price to cover the repair?

Though unexpected faults in the house can cause Excedrin headaches, they can also serve as valuable negotiating tools. Say an inspection has uncovered a $2,000 problem in the heating system and you and the sellers sit $4,000 apart in the price charged versus price offered for the home. The sellers, in their counteroffer, have agreed to fix the heating system.

You are buying this house in April. You know the local climate and figure that you won't need to use the heat until October. By then, you will have been able to save up the $2,000 needed for repair. You may want to rewrite your offer saying that you'll

Minor Home Repairs

Any home on which you bid will likely need a number of picayune repairs that you're really not going to bother asking the seller to make. Who would risk losing a house over a loose doorknob or creaking floorboard?

Because you probably don't have tons of money to throw around, you might want to consider tackling these jobs yourself. You can buy home repair books (often given their own section in large bookstores) or you can get online and find much of the same information for free.

Two good Web sites where you can learn more about home repair are http://www.ourbroker.com and http://www.hometime.com. Our Broker offers a plethora of home repair information and contains links to similar sites. HomeTime serves up more of the same and also acts as the online companion to the popular PBS series of the same name.

fix the heating system if the sellers drop their price to meet your bid. They'll realize that they are only "losing" $2,000 (because they have saved on repair costs) and you'll be left with a house you can afford.

Recognizing When You Have a Good Deal

If you realize, through your research, that the sellers have listed their house at a rock-bottom price, don't haggle too much. If a $100,000 price tag represents a terrific bargain, don't write an offer for $90,000. You'll insult the sellers. They may tell you to buzz off. Sure, you might want to proffer $98,000 or $99,000 just to try your luck. But if the owners hold fast, don't let a grand or two keep you from getting a great deal on a great house.

Loading, or the Nonnegotiating Negotiation

Prospective buyers and real estate agents often use a technique called *loading* to nudge reluctant sellers into accepting a fair and reasonable offer for their home. The process entails listing, in polite but clear language, comparable properties in the area that have sold for less than your prospective new home. You can load your first offer. You can also use the technique to rev up stalled negotiations. Here's how it works.

You write a letter to the sellers and attach it to your offer. You start with a polite paragraph or two explaining that you like the house and that you want to offer them a fair price. You then list other, comparable properties in the area that have recently sold. Include their addresses, their original list prices, and their actual sale prices. Make sure that each property you choose to list has a feature or amenity lacking in the home you have offered to buy. These amenities can include:

- A larger or more attractive lot

- New carpeting, new heating/cooling system, new roof, and so on

- A patio or deck

- A pool or hot tub

- Larger closets

- A three-car garage

- Major appliances

- Anything else you can think of

This part of your letter can help the sellers realize that if a three-bedroom home with a pool in their neighborhood sold for $112,000, it is unreasonable for them to demand $118,000 for a similar home sans pool.

In the second part of your letter, include all the comparable properties that sellers have listed in the area. Include list price, address, and, again, a list of amenities that each of these properties offer that your seller's home does not. This is a not-so-subtle way of letting the sellers know that, should they reject your offer, you have other options.

Next, list both your assets as a buyer and any concessions that you are willing to make to bring the sale to fruition. These can include:

- Your preapproval for a loan

- Your willingness to put off closing for a month or two until the seller is able to move

- For first-time homebuyers, the fact that your purchase of this home is not contingent on selling yours first

- Your willingness to pay for certain home repairs

- Your willingness to allow the sellers to take certain fixtures or major appliances with them when they move

After the paragraph outlining your strong points, again note that you look forward to paying a fair price for the home. Say what that fair price is. Then state that this is either your first and only bid or, if you've been negotiating with the seller, your final bid. Add that you are unable to consider a counteroffer on the seller's part. Conclude by saying you look forward to an early close.

Some might consider this technique a little hardball, but really, it's not. You used polite language when you wrote this letter, and all you did was outline the facts of the situation. The sellers can either accept or reject your offer. If they accept it, terrific. If not, move on.

When to Walk Away

Disappointing as it may be, sometimes you have no choice but to walk away from your negotiations. You can do this without fear of losing your earnest money as long as certain circumstances are met (see the sidebar on page 94).

When It's OK to Walk Away from Negotiations

You have probably put up some earnest money and no doubt wonder: If negotiations stall, when can I walk away and still get my cash back? Remember it this way: You are only bound by the offers you proffer.

You are bound to your initial bid for its duration. (Offers are usually written to last for only a day or two.) If the seller accepts the deal, you either carry through with your promise or lose your earnest money. If the seller counters your offer, you are no longer bound to anything and you can walk away without financial reprisals.

If you counter the seller's offer, you are again bound to your bid for its duration. In short, whoever makes the offer or counteroffer is bound to it. The person to whom the offer is made is not under any obligation whatsoever.

You can also feel free to pull out of negotiations if your contingencies haven't been met—for example, if the house fails inspection.

You may decide to leave the table if offers and counteroffers have been flying fast and furious without their terms changing significantly enough to make either side happy. The emotional toll this can take on both you and the seller is substantial. Sometimes you'll find it easier just to start looking for another home.

These types of situations often arise when either party proves unreasonable. But before you walk away cursing an unreasonable seller, you might want to ask a few questions about your own ability to bend.

- Have you come in with a ridiculously lowball offer and then been disappointed when the seller has refused to accept it?

- Have you fallen in love with an antique crystal chandelier and refuse to buy the house without it, even though it belonged to the seller's great-great grandmother?

- Are you willing to let a house you love go because the owner refuses to recarpet the living room?

Sellers are often emotional and unreasonable. You should keep cool—and be flexible when necessary.

Top Five Things to Do Right Now

1. Reexamine your relationship with your agent. If you have chosen to work with a buyer's broker, terrific. If you have chosen to work with a seller's agent, remember that the law may require that agent to pass on to the seller any tidbit learned about you, as well as your negotiating strategy.

2. Adopt a win-win attitude toward negotiations with the seller.

3. Learn as much as you can about the seller and about comparable sales in the neighborhood.

4. Examine the counteroffer proffered by the seller. If it's a deal you're willing to accept, fine. If you're unable to pay the seller's price, examine areas of negotiation that may nudge the seller into lowering the cost of the home without your paying more money up front.

5. Decide how you want to hold title to your home.

Choosing the RIGHT *Mortgage*

CHAPTER SEVEN

A *little loan hunting can save you thousands of dollars in up-front fees and tens of thousands of dollars over the life of the mortgage.*

Too many buyers spend weeks bickering with the seller over a $1,000 difference in the sales price but then make the mistake of spending only a few hours searching for the best financing package to close the deal.

Not long ago, searching for a loan to finance a purchase was an easy task. Lenders offered only fixed-rate mortgages, and the only real choice borrowers faced was whether they wanted to pay the money back over 30 or 15 years.

That's not the case today. As a buyer, you'll face a dizzying array of mortgage choices. There are loans with interest rates that go up and down monthly, loans that start with a below-market rate that gradually climbs, even loans that require you to pay "interest only" until you're ready to sell and move again. There are "no points" loans

that cost almost nothing to get, or special programs that offer ultralow rates if you've got a sizable down payment. There are special plans for self-employed people, and even loan plans designed to help you qualify for a loan if you, er, "fudged" a bit on reporting how much money you made when you filed your last tax return.

The array of loan options available today gives you an unprecedented opportunity to match your particular borrowing needs and housing plans with a mortgage that could save you tens or even hundreds of thousands of dollars over the next several years. But wading through all the options can be a laborious task and you can't be blamed if you wind up feeling like a mouse running through a maze. This chapter will help you avoid bumping into walls as you negotiate the mortgage maze in search of that perfect little cheese ball—the mortgage that's best for you.

Different Types of Lenders

There are plenty of people willing to loan you money to buy a house. You're probably most familiar with banks and savings and loans. In fact, you probably already have your checking account, savings account, or certificate of deposit with them. Another common source of financing is mortgage bankers, which are institutions that specialize in making home loans and usually don't provide other types of services.

At the risk of making a sweeping generalization, mortgage bankers tend to offer some of the lowest mortgage rates available. That's largely because they aren't stuck with the overhead of operating an extensive network of offices, like many banks and S&Ls do. But now that we've made one broad generalization, here's another: Mortgage bankers often don't provide the type of personalized service—or long menu of services—that many banks and S&Ls do. That could be an important factor in your decision about which lender to use, especially if you're happy with the service that your current bank or S&L provides.

As you start looking for a mortgage, don't overlook the possibility of financing your purchase with the help of a credit union. Credit unions tend to offer the lowest rates of all because their nonprofit status allows them the freedom of not having to worry about providing shareholders with huge returns on their investments.

Banks and other traditional lenders have long envied the special tax treatment that credit unions enjoy. They've been working hard to take that tax-exempt status away or, at least, to prevent credit unions from accepting new members. But you can probably still find a credit union that you can join if you don't belong to one already. Most large employers and even many small ones offer their workers access to a credit union, so call your company's employee benefits department to see if one is available. Many professional organizations, trade unions, alumni associations, and even big churches and synagogues provide their members with credit union access. If your parents belong to a credit union, there's a good chance you can join it, too. Not all credit unions issue mortgages, but those that do offer some of the best deals.

VISIT THE WEB

The nonprofit Credit Union National Association offers a free service to help you find a credit union you can join in your area. Visit its Web site (http://www.cuna.org) or call its toll-free number (800-358-5710) for more information.

Working with a Mortgage Broker

When you call or visit a bank, the loan representative you talk to will be happy to tell you about all the different mortgage plans that it has available. But obviously, the rep's not going to tell you about the plans and rates offered by other institutions in the area. No rep gets paid to refer you to competitors, even if he or she knows they offer a better deal. That's why it's so important for you to call at least three local banks, three S&Ls, three mortgage bankers, and at least one credit union as you start your search for the best available financing. It takes a little time, but it's the only way to ensure that you have a truly accurate picture of what different lenders are charging. Knocking a mere one-quarter of one percentage point off your loan rate can save you more than $7,000 in finance charges over the life of a $125,000, 30-year mortgage. If that's not worth spending a few hours looking for the best deal, what is?

Though doing your own legwork is important, it's equally important to visit one or two local mortgage brokers as you hunt for the perfect mortgage. Unlike a loan rep who works for a bank or S&L, a good mortgage broker has the authority to repre-

sent several different lenders and can offer the same financing plans you'd get if you worked directly with those lenders yourself.

How the Broker Is Paid

You usually don't have to pay any money to use a mortgage broker. Instead, the broker is paid by the lender who eventually issues your loan. Rather than keeping all your up-front fees for itself, the lender will give some of the money to the broker as compensation for handling your mortgage application and doing most of the other work that the lender would otherwise have to do itself. Federal law generally prohibits brokers from collecting an up-front fee for their own services, but it's perfectly legal for them to demand that you pay for a credit report and a few other expenses in advance.

Some tips for finding a good mortgage broker are provided in the sidebar below. Although enlisting the help of at least one broker is a good idea, remember that the broker's efforts are only a supplement—not a substitute—for doing your own loan legwork. Contacting several lenders yourself and buttressing your search with a good broker is the best way to ensure that you get the best rate and other terms to finance your loan purchase.

How to Find a Good Mortgage Broker

Good mortgage brokers, like good real estate agents, are worth their weight in gold. Bad ones aren't worth their weight in beetle dung. Relatives, friends, and neighbors who have recently purchased a house or refinanced a loan are among your best sources of referrals. Here are some key questions to ask when you call or visit a broker:

- *How long have you been in business?* The best mortgage brokers have been in business full-time for at least a few years, which is the minimum time it takes to establish good working relationships with lenders.

- *What's your license number?* Virtually all states require brokers to hold a real estate license or similar permit. Call the issuing agency to make sure the license is valid and ask the agency how to check to see if the broker has been subject to disciplinary action in the past.

- *How many lenders do you work with regularly?* A good broker represents three or even more than a half-dozen lenders. The more lenders a broker represents, the more loan options that broker can offer you.

- *How will you be paid for helping me?* Most brokers don't charge borrowers a nickel for their services, but instead collect a fee from the lender who issues the loan. Make sure a broker promises that working with that broker won't increase the fees or loan rate you'd pay if you worked with the broker's lenders directly.

- *What kind of financing plan should I choose?* A good broker won't answer this question without first getting some details about your personal financial situation, including the amount of money you've saved for a down payment, your income, and your current debt. If the broker makes a recommendation without asking for such important data first, it's a sign that broker is either lazy or is merely telling you what he or she thinks you want to hear. Either way, that broker doesn't deserve your business.

Basic Loan Types

There are more than 20,000 banks and S&Ls in the country, plus another 15,000 or so credit unions and mortgage bankers. Figuring that each of them offer maybe six different loan plans, you technically have more than 200,000 mortgage options.

There's an old adage that says, "Anyone who thinks too long about all the stars in the universe will go crazy." As a first-time buyer, it might seem like there are more mortgage plans than there are stars in the cosmos. It'll help you keep your sanity if you understand that all those loan plans that different lenders offer really fall into one of three simple categories: fixed-rate loans, adjustable-rate mortgages (ARMs), and hybrid loans that are a cross between fixed-rate loans and ARMs.

Deciding which of the three loan types is best for you is a fairly easy task. You'll probably have your mind made up about five minutes from now—after you've read the next couple of pages. Determining the kind of loan you want will also mark the halfway point of your search for the perfect mortgage. Negotiating the mortgage maze isn't so difficult after all, is it?

Door Number 1: Fixed-Rate Loans

Fixed-rate loans are the easiest kind of loans to understand: The lender gives you a fixed interest rate that will never change, which means your monthly payments won't change either. With fixed interest rates in 1999 far below their historic average, you can't be blamed if you've already decided that a fixed-rate loan is best for you.

Before you march out to a lender and choose a fixed-rate loan, at least consider the drawbacks. The low rate a lender offers you today may seem like a terrific bargain, but it won't look so good if mortgage rates drop again—a very real possibility as the economy slows and talk about a looming recession grows louder. People who choose adjustable-rate mortgages will automatically benefit if rates drop, but the only way you could take advantage of another rate decline is to suffer the hassle and cost of refinancing your fixed-rate mortgage.

While fixed rates are fairly low today, it's also important to realize that introductory rates on ARMs are even lower. Sure, an ARM's low introductory rate will begin float-

ing up toward fixed-rate levels after a few months or a year or two. But first-time buyers tend to move sooner than other buyers do, which means an ARM could be a better choice because its low rate will save you money in the early years of the loan and you might move again before the rate has a chance to ratchet too far upward. Many adjustable-rate plans also feature options that let you reduce your monthly payments if you lose a job, run into unexpected bills, or need to earmark more cash for home improvements or tuition fees. Choosing a fixed-rate loan doesn't give you any flexibility: If you can't meet the preset monthly payment, the lender can begin foreclosure proceedings.

In the end, a fixed-rate loan is your best choice if you want to ensure that your payments will never change, you plan to live in the house for at least three years, and you have some extra cash set aside to meet the loan's rigid repayment requirements even if you lose your job or run into unexpected expenses. If you don't meet at least two of those three criteria, seriously consider choosing an ARM or hybrid loan.

Door Number 2: The ARM

Adjustable-rate mortgages haven't been very popular among buyers over the past few years as fixed interest rates dropped near the lowest levels in a generation. Even though many lenders are offering some terrific fixed-rate mortgages today, choosing an ARM instead may provide you with some important benefits.

First, introductory rates on ARMs—the rate you'll pay when you first take out the loan—are almost always two or three percentage points lower than the rate you'd pay if you insist on a fixed-rate mortgage. If you need to borrow $100,000 over 30 years and you're offered a 7.5 percent fixed rate or a 5 percent adjustable, choosing the ARM will initially save you $163 a month. That's an important point to consider if you're already strapped for cash and your budget will get even tighter after you move into your new home.

Keeping your payments in the first years of your mortgage low by choosing an ARM rather than a fixed-rate loan can provide other benefits. Because your initial housing expenses will be lower if you pick an ARM, the lender will likely be willing to loan you more money than you'd get if you chose a fixed-rate loan. The ARM will gobble

up less of your take-home pay and thus reduce the chances that you'll default. The ability to borrow more money by choosing an ARM over a fixed-rate loan could allow you to buy a nicer home in a better neighborhood. Many lenders will also reduce their down payment requirements, waive many of their fees, and even loosen their borrowing standards for buyers who will accept an ARM.

Of course, the biggest risk involved in choosing an ARM to finance your purchase is that the interest rate on your loan—and thus your monthly payment—will change as time passes. If rates go down, so will your payment. But if rates go up, your payments will rise too. Paying an extra $100 or even more each month because your ARM rate is adjusted upward won't be a big problem if you expect your income to keep rising over the next several years. But even a modest $25 per month increase could be tough to handle if you lose your job, your spouse doesn't work, you have to make a big tuition payment for your kid, or you run into unexpectedly big bills.

A Call to ARMs?

Fixed mortgage rates are near their 25-year lows, but choosing an adjustable-rate mortgage can still provide you with important benefits. Qualifying for an ARM is usually easier, you can borrow more money than you could with a fixed-rate loan, and your set-up fees may be lower too. Here are some questions to ask a lender before you answer the "call to ARMs":

- *How often will my rate be adjusted?* Rates on some ARMs are adjusted only once or twice, while others are adjusted monthly. But most call for adjustments to be made once every 6 or 12 months. The more time between adjustment periods, the less you have to worry about fluctuating payments.

- *What index is used to make adjustments?* All ARMs are based on an index that determines whether your new rate will rise or fall. Some indexes, such as the common one-year Treasury index, change fairly quickly. Others, including the popular Cost of Funds Index (COFI), tend to move much more slowly. Choosing a slow-moving index will reduce the chance that you'll be subject to wide swings in your payment each time the rate is adjusted.

• *What's the ARM's margin?* The *margin* is basically the lender's retail markup on the loan. If the index rate is 5.5 percent and the margin is two-and-one-half percentage points, the rate that you'll be charged is 8 percent.

• *Is there a rate adjustment cap?* A good ARM will have a limit, or "cap," that prevents your loan rate from rising more than one or two percentage points at each adjustment period. That's an important feature because it will keep your payments from swinging wildly each time the rate is adjusted.

• *What's the life-of-loan cap?* A life-of-loan cap will prevent your rate from rising above a certain level regardless of how long you keep your mortgage. The best caps keep your rate from climbing more than 5 or 6 percent over the life of the loan. If your ARM starts with a 5 percent rate and has a five point lifetime cap, the rate you pay can never exceed 10 percent even if overall interest rates skyrocket several years from now.

• *Does the ARM have the potential for negative amortization?* Negative amortization occurs when rate or payment caps on your loan prevent the lender from increasing your future payments to a point where they can cover both the principal and interest that's owed on your mortgage. The result: Your loan balance actually grows larger rather than smaller with every payment you make. Ask the lender or mortgage broker if the loan you're considering has the potential for negative amortization, and to explain the ramifications if it does.

Choose an ARM if you need to keep your expenses as low as possible in the early years of the loan, you plan to move again before the rate can move a lot higher, or you don't meet the more rigid criteria lenders use to qualify for a fixed-rate loan. Select a fixed-rate or hybrid loan instead if you expect to live in the home for at least three or five years, you'd have a difficult time meeting your obligations if your housing payments climbed, or you couldn't sleep at night knowing that your interest rate is subject to frequent changes.

Door Number 3: The Hybrid Mortgage

Hybrid loans are one part fixed rate and one part adjustable. Most start with a fixed interest rate that's guaranteed for a preset period, usually between one and five years. After the fixed-rate term expires, the loan becomes an ARM. In some types of hybrid loans, only one adjustment is made and the rate stays at that new level for the remainder of the loan term. Other hybrids call for more frequent adjustments, which means your payments will fall if rates drop. But if rates climb, your payments will also climb.

If you can't decide whether to select a fixed-rate loan or conventional ARM, choosing a hybrid loan can be a happy compromise. The most common hybrid loans are explained in the following sidebar.

Hybrid Loans

If you can't decide on a fixed-rate loan or ARM, you can always choose a hybrid mortgage that combines their features. Below are brief descriptions of some common hybrids and their respective attributes.

Two-Step Loans

These loans start with a below-market fixed rate that's good for a preset period, usually five or seven years. Then comes a one-time rate

adjustment. If rates have moved lower since you took the loan out, your own rate and payments will fall. If rates have gone up, your rate and payments go up too. Either way, the new rate will stay in effect for the life of the loan.

Choose a two-step loan if you want an initial rate that's below those charged on conventional fixed-rate loans but can't stomach the thought of taking an ARM whose rate will adjust several times over the life of the mortgage.

Balloon Loans

Most balloons work like two-steps, except your initial fixed rate is even lower. The catch: You must pay off the entire balance with a huge lump-sum "balloon" payment at the end of five or seven years. Unless you've hit the lottery, you'll probably have to sell the home or spend money to refinance in order to pay the loan off.

Choose a balloon loan if you want an extremely low fixed rate in the early years of the loan and are almost certain that you'll move by the time the balloon payment comes due.

Graduated-Payment Mortgages

Most GPMs start with a below-market fixed rate that rises to preset levels at preset periods. For example, your contract might call for an ultralow 5 percent fixed rate in the first year, rising to 6 percent in the second year, 7 percent in the third, and 8 percent for the fourth year and beyond. It's hard to find a lender who makes GPMs, but it'll be worth the extra effort if you want to start with a below-market rate and know exactly when—and by how much—your future payments will rise.

Choose a GPM if you want to start with a below-market fixed rate but do not want to cope with the uncertainty of a traditional ARM. A GPM may be especially attractive if you expect your income to rise faster than your preset mortgage payments or if you plan to move again before the GPM's rate reaches its maximum level.

Alternative Financing

Buying a Home without Much Cash

Many first-time buyers mistakenly think they need at least a 10 or 20 percent down payment to purchase a home. In reality, there are several ways to purchase a home with a mere 5 percent down payment—or sometimes even less.

FHA loans. The Federal Housing Administration has helped more than 100 million people purchase a home since it was created during the Depression. The FHA's most popular plan allows you to purchase a home with a 5 percent down payment. If you live in a rural area where prices aren't very high, you might need to put down a mere 3 percent. The FHA doesn't make loans directly to buyers. Instead, you must visit an FHA-approved lender and the lender will obtain an insurance policy from the FHA that will cover its losses if you fail to pay the money back. You can get more information about FHA loans by calling a few mortgage brokers in your area or by contacting the nearest regional office of its parent agency, the U.S. Department of Housing and Urban Development. Or visit HUD's Web site on the Internet (http://www.hud.gov).

VA loans. Millions of veterans who served in our nation's armed forces qualify for low-rate, no-down-payment loans insured by the U.S. Department of Veterans Affairs. Many reservists and members of the national guard qualify for the loans, as do virtually all vets who have served in the Army, Navy, Air Force, or Marines. Like the FHA, the VA doesn't make loans directly to buyers. Instead, you must visit a VA-approved lender or mortgage broker who will handle all the required paperwork and obtain a loan guarantee that will cover the lender's losses if you eventually default. You can get a list of approved lenders in your area by contacting the nearest regional office of the U.S. Department of Veterans Affairs, which you can probably find under the "U.S. Government" heading of the white pages in your phone book. Or visit the VA's outstanding Internet Web site (http://www.va.gov) for answers to frequently asked questions about the program and other important details.

Fannie Mae and Freddie Mac loans. Two quasi-government agencies that we discussed earlier, Fannie Mae and Freddie Mac, operate special loan plans for first-time buyers that require down payments of 5 percent or less. The best way to find out about the

plans they offer in your particular area is to contact the agencies directly. Fannie Mae's toll-free number is 800-732-6643 and its Web address is http:www.fanniemae.com. Freddie Mac's toll-free line is 800-424-5401 and it can be reached on the Web at http://www.freddiemac.com.

Conventional low down payment mortgages. Several lenders have recently introduced new mortgage plans tailored to the special needs of first-time buyers. Many require a mere 3 or 5 percent down payment, plus generous loan-qualifying standards that make it easier to get the money you need to buy your first home. The best way to find out what's available in your chosen neighborhood is to contact one or two mortgage brokers, and then supplement their information by calling a few lenders in the area yourself.

How Seller Financing Works

What happens if you choose a home but the bank won't give you a loan that's big enough to complete the purchase? You might still be able to close the deal if you can persuade the seller to provide the rest of the needed financing.

Seller financing typically involves the use of a second mortgage—called a *take back* or *carry back*—that the seller agrees to make as part of the sales transaction.

Say you have a $10,000 down payment and you want to buy a $100,000 home. You need to borrow $90,000 to complete the purchase but the bank will lend you only $75,000 because you don't earn enough to qualify for the full $90,000.

To close the deal, the sellers could agree to carry back (take back) a second mortgage for $15,000—the amount needed to fill the gap between the $75,000 first mortgage the bank will issue and the $90,000 you must borrow to complete the purchase.

Instead of making one mortgage payment each month, you'd have to make two. The first check would go to the lender who financed the bulk of your purchase price. The other check, which would be much smaller, would go to the sellers as payment toward the $15,000 second mortgage they carried back so you could purchase their house.

Both you and the sellers could benefit from this arrangement. You would get to buy the house even though the bank wouldn't finance the entire purchase, while the sellers would avoid the necessity of putting their home back on the market. The sellers would also collect interest on the second mortgage they provided you and would have the safety of knowing they could foreclose and retake possession of the home in the unlikely event that you quit paying.

Getting Help from Your Relatives

By some estimates, nearly one-third of all first-time buyers get some sort of financial help from their parents. Below are the three basic types of assistance that parents or other relatives can provide, followed by "inside tips" from lenders to help you secure the mortgage you need.

- *A cash gift toward the down payment.* Some lucky buyers get outright gifts from their folks or other relatives to make a down payment on their first home. If you're among those fortunate few, the lender will likely ask that your folks sign a "gift letter" stating that the money is truly a gift with no strings attached, rather than a loan that must be repaid. If your relatives say they'll give you some of the cash to buy a new home, it's wise to have them write you a check as soon as possible. Lenders always check the average balance of your checking and savings accounts for the past three or six months when they begin processing your loan application. By depositing your parents' check now, you'll raise that average and improve your chances of getting a loan even if you don't expect to submit a formal loan application for another month or two.

- *A loan to help you make a down payment.* Most parents simply don't have enough money to *give* their kids some down payment cash. So, mom and pop *loan* the money instead. Some lenders will get nervous if your loan application indicates that some of your down payment cash will come from a parental loan instead of an outright gift. Making payments on the bank's first mortgage will be hard enough, so the lender may be particularly wary about your ability to make the payments on the bank's mortgage if you'll also be saddled with payments on a loan from your folks. Talk to the lender about your plans to get a loan from your relatives *before* you submit a formal application to the bank. There's no sense in completing all the paperwork and paying up-front charges for a credit report and other services if the lender's in-house policies will prevent you from getting a loan simply because you have to borrow some of your down payment.

- *Cosigning your loan application.* Getting cash from your loved ones for a down payment on a house is nice but, in some cases, getting them to cosign your loan application is even better. When relatives agree to cosign your mortgage application, they essentially promise to make your monthly home loan payments if you can't (or won't) make the payments yourself. They're tapping the strength of the good credit record they have personally built over the past several years and transferring that strength to you, the first-time homebuyer. Your chances of gaining loan approval will likely skyrocket if your parents or other relatives cosign your application. But all the cosigners in the world won't help you get a mortgage if your cosigners have financial problems of their own or major blemishes on their own credit record.

A "Pointed" Decision

We've already mentioned loan points—the prepaid interest charges you must pay to a lender to get a mortgage. One point is equal to 1 percent of the total loan amount. If you need a $120,000 loan and agree to pay one-and-one-half points, your points would cost you $1,800 ($120,000 x 0.015 = $1,800). The more points you pay, the lower your interest rate will be.

You Control the Points

It's important to understand that you, not the lender, usually have the power to determine how many points you'll pay. If you expect to live in your new home for at least five to seven years, it might make sense to pay three or even five points because the monthly savings you'll enjoy by getting a rock-bottom interest rate will easily offset your up-front expenses. But if you plan to move again within a few years, you should probably look for a zero points loan or a lender that would charge only one point. Paying several points to get the lowest possible rate would be foolish if you don't expect to hang around long enough for your monthly savings to offset the points you paid to get the mortgage.

Other "Pointers"

- Many lenders will let you combine your points into your new loan amount. Say you want a $150,000 loan and are willing to pay two points ($3,000). The lender may be willing to raise your loan amount to $153,000 to cover the cost of your points, essentially allowing you to pay the costs as part of your monthly installments instead of paying them in cash when the loan is first issued.

- Paying cash for your points will affect your down payment. The points you pay can reduce the size of your down payment. Again, say you want a $150,000 loan and you must pay the lender $3,000 in points. If you can't combine the points into your total loan amount, you'll have to pay the full $3,000 in cash before the loan is issued. That shouldn't be a problem if you've got plenty of money to make a down payment and to cover your closing costs. But if you don't have a lot of cash, paying the $3,000 up front will mean you'll have $3,000 less for the down payment—which could leave you penniless after you move into the house or even prevent you from qualifying for a mortgage to buy it.

- Points are tax deductible. If you pay your points in cash when you take out the loan, you can deduct the entire cost of the points when you file your next tax return. But if you combine the points into your total loan amount, you'll get to take only a partial deduction on your next return and have to write off the remainder of the cost—bit by bit—over each of the next several years.

Other Loan Fees

Any points you agree to pay will almost certainly be your biggest single loan-related expense. But lenders have recently become extremely creative in dreaming up new ways to levy questionable charges on their loan applicants. Those charges can easily add hundreds or even thousands of dollars to the cost of getting a mortgage.

There are some fees that are almost impossible to avoid. For example, all lenders will require that the property you want to purchase be inspected by an appraiser before your loan application is approved. The lender needs to ensure that you don't borrow more money than the home is really worth, and getting the opinion of a professional appraiser is the only way it can do that. Similarly, no lender is going to give you a loan without first checking your credit history.

Appraisers, credit reporting bureaus, and all the other people or companies involved in the loan process charge for their services. A few lenders will pay many of the charges themselves, but most expect you to pay for them. It's important to ask each lender you visit exactly what fees you'll be charged. Ask for a written list of all the fees before you file your application. It's the only way you can be sure to have the cash available to pay them when closing day arrives.

Taking Out the Garbage (Fees)

While some fees cannot be avoided, lenders will often reduce or completely waive certain other charges—but only if you ask them to. These so-called "garbage fees" are often listed on the preprinted closing cost worksheets that lenders use, so first-time buyers frequently make the mistake of thinking the costs are nonnegotiable. But when push comes to shove, many lenders are willing to drop them. Reducing or waiving some fees might cost them some money now, but lenders know it's a small price to pay for the tens of thousands of dollars they'll make off your interest payments over the next several years.

The typical fees that many lenders are willing to reduce or eliminate are listed below. But remember, they won't be cut unless you ask. The worst the lender can do is say "no."

- *Document preparation fee.* Many lenders charge $200 or more for "doc prep" fees. That's ridiculous because all they need to do is hit the print button on their computer to generate the paperwork. Ask for a waiver.

- *Processing fee.* Another garbage fee. Get it waived and save up to $200.

- *Loan underwriting fee.* This fee can range from as little as $100 to more than $500. You can usually get it eliminated or reduced, especially if you have a fairly simple transaction.

- *Warehouse fee.* Another silly fee that supposedly reimburses the lender for "warehousing" your loan money until closing day arrives. Get it waived to save up to $300.

- *Appraisal review fee.* This fee, which can cost $200 or more, shouldn't be charged unless the initial appraisal comes in too low and the lender needs to reexamine the report or the property itself.

- *Courier fees.* Couriers charge up to $50 for each trip they make to shuttle paperwork back and forth between the lender, title company, escrow holder, and the like. You can save hundreds of dollars if you tell the lender up front that you want to use the U.S. Postal Service whenever possible or that you're willing to hand deliver the documents yourself.

- *Notary fees.* Notaries public typically charge between $10 and $20 for each document they're asked to notarize. But most lenders have an in-house notary, and you shouldn't be charged for their services any more than you should be charged for having a teller take a deposit. Have the fees waived.

- *Settlement fees and other closing costs.* This is a catchall category that lenders often use to pile on even more fees that can total hundreds or even more than $1,000. The lender may be willing to negotiate a reduction. The seller, too, is often willing to help with these expenses—but only if you ask for such help when you negotiate the sales contract.

The Length of Your New Loan

Most borrowers who take out a new loan—whether they're buying a house or simply refinancing an existing mortgage—automatically choose a repayment plan that will pay off the lender in 30 years. A typical 30-year mortgage has some distinct advantages over its shorter-term counterparts, but it also has some drawbacks.

The beauty of a 30-year repayment plan is that it will keep your monthly payments to a minimum because the money you borrow will be paid back over the longest period of time possible. That's particularly important if you're strapped for cash or if you would have trouble qualifying for the slightly higher payments that a shorter-term mortgage would entail. On the downside, a 30-year term means it'll take longer to build equity in your home and interest payments over the life of the loan will be far higher than you would pay if you chose a loan with a shorter repayment schedule.

Shorter Is Better

Consider this example: If you took out a fixed-rate, 30-year mortgage for $100,000 at 8 percent, your monthly payment for principal and interest would be about $734. If you kept the mortgage for the entire 30 years, you would pay a staggering $164,149 in interest over the life of the loan plus the $100,000 you originally borrowed.

If you instead chose a 15-year term, your interest rate would probably be about 7.5 percent because rates on 15-year loans are usually about one-half of a percentage

point below rates on 30-year loans. Your monthly payment on the 15-year plan would be $927, roughly 20 percent more that you'd pay if you selected a 30-year schedule. However, your long-term finance charges under the 15-year program would drop to $66,861. In other words, paying an extra $193 a month would allow you to own your home free and clear in half the usual time and slash your long-term interest charges by nearly 60 percent. Wouldn't it be nice to pay your loan off before you retire or your kids start for college, while saving nearly $100,000 in the process?

In short, you should probably choose a 30-year term if you want to keep your payments as low as possible or if you'd have trouble qualifying for the higher monthly payments that a shorter-term loan would require. But if you'd like to pay your loan off much sooner and save tens of thousands in interest, seriously consider the benefits that choosing a 10-, 15-, or 20-year repayment term could provide.

Top Five Things to Do Right Now

1. Call or visit at least three local banks, three S&Ls, and three mortgage bankers to see what kind of loan plans they have available. It should take no more than a day of your time, and choosing the best plan could literally save you thousands in closing costs and tens of thousands over the life of the loan.

2. Call the National Credit Union Association (800-358-5710) or visit its Web site (http://www.cuna.org) to see if you can join a credit union (if you don't already belong to one). Credit unions often offer the best home financing programs available.

3. Ask relatives, friends, neighbors, and your real estate agent to recommend a mortgage broker they trust. But remember, using a broker is a way to supplement your search for the perfect mortgage, not a substitute for making your own calls and doing your own legwork.

4. Familiarize yourself with the advantages and drawbacks of the three basic types of loans: fixed-rate mortgages, ARMs, and hybrids. Lenders and mortgage brokers you talk to can help you decide which type of loan is best for you.

5. Remember that lenders are willing to negotiate for your business. You can save hundreds or even thousands of dollars if you can persuade the lender to waive or reduce a mere handful of its fees. If you've got a sterling credit record and can make a sizable down payment, you're in a strong position to get a slight rate discount and other concessions, as well.

GETTING Ready for Closing DAY

The closing is, simply, the meeting of the minds, the moment where the seller relieves you of all of your money—papers are signed, title is transferred, many checks are written—and at the end, the house is yours.

Your real estate agent has undoubtedly discussed with you all the closing costs you'll have to pay. Closing costs are the fees—excluding the down payment—that you pay before assuming ownership of your new digs. The phrase, though, is a little misleading. It implies that you'll pay all these fees on closing day.

Not true. You've probably already paid some of these bills, such as those associated with having your home inspected and those charged by the lender when you applied for a loan. Your seller should have already incurred a few fees also, notably for supplying you with a warranty to protect against unforeseen problems with the house. (See chapter 9 for details.)

But there are still other costs you'll incur well before the big day.

For example, your lender will demand that you bring to the closing a receipt for payment of homeowners insurance and, possibly, for mortgage insurance. Clearly, you need to have purchased these policies before you sign the deed.

In addition to all the financial concerns rolling around inside your head, you'll also need to consider the logistics of your move. How do you plan to lug all your stuff from your old place to your new place? It's now time to call the movers or any friends who'll lend a hand for the price of some beer and a pizza. And because you don't want to spend the first night in your new home stumbling around in the dark, take some time to contact your new electric company.

Think of the rest of this chapter as a giant checklist outlining what you need to do and buy in preparation for your close and move. You will also learn when these chores must be completed. You can put off some purchases until closing day. Other things must be bought well before then.

Preparing for the Close

Before closing day comes you'll need to buy insurance and tour your soon-to-be home one more time.

Before you close your lender will mail you a commitment letter. Basically this letter states that, yeah, the institution has agreed to lend you the mortgage bucks you need. But it also makes that commitment contingent on certain demands. For example, your bank will expect you to buy homeowners insurance. The lender may also want to ensure that you have made certain repairs to your home.

The following is a general list of what you may have to buy before you close. Use it as a guideline only. Consider your commitment letter your bible.

What to Buy

- *Homeowners insurance, casualty and liability.* Casualty insurance covers your home in case of robbery or natural disaster. Liability insurance protects against accidents on your property (someone slipping, falling, and breaking a leg in your front yard, etc.). Your lender will require that you prepay one year's worth of premiums for this coverage and the bank will tell you how much protection it demands. (Lenders will often ask that you insure the property for an amount equal to the sale price minus the value of the land on which your new home sits.) However, you may want to invest in a more comprehensive policy, insuring the house at its replacement value and covering all your possessions. Shop around for rates, talking to reputable insurance agents. You can also do some research on the Net at sites such as http://www.thehartford.com or http://www.statefarm.com.

- *Mortgage insurance.* If you have offered a down payment of less than 20 percent of the price of your new house, or if you have an FHA loan, your lender will demand that you purchase mortgage insurance. This insurance protects the institution's interest in the event that you renege on your loan. Premiums paid for mortgage insurance on FHA loans are referred to as *mortgage insurance premiums,* or MIP; for conventional loans, *private mortgage insurance,* or PMI.

- *Title insurance.* This protection shields the lender from unexpected ownership claims against the property. In some states, you are expected to purchase this one-payment policy before closing. In other areas, you secure it on closing day.

- *Anything else demanded by your lender's letter of commitment.* As noted earlier, your lender will mail you a letter of commitment outlining the institution's monetary promises to you. These promises are contingent on certain demands. In addition to the homeowners, mortgage, and title insurances outlined above, the lender may require you to buy other protections, such as flood insurance if your new home is located on a flood plain. The lender may also demand that you perform certain repairs on the home before closing day.

PREPARING FOR WET WEATHER

Live in a floodplain? You may find that, in some areas of the country, flood insurance is becoming increasingly hard to get. Call the National Flood Insurance Program at 800-638-6200 to get information on available policies.

Don't Forget the Final Walk-Through

One or two days before you close, you and your agent need to tour your soon-to-be home—your "final walk-through." You need to ensure that the home's current owners are leaving the property in the condition in which you agreed to buy it. That means, for example, that they didn't throw a drunken "we finally sold our house party," during which some rowdy friends punched their fists through the drywall; that they haven't decided to leave, in the middle of the living room, all the junk they're too tired to move; and that they haven't already transported their washer-dryer to their new digs, "forgetting" that they were included in the sale price.

Remember this: While it's possible that the owner may be willing to fix problems after the close, don't bet on it. You should either refuse to close until any serious flaws in the home are repaired or demand that a percentage of the purchase price be held in escrow until the repairs are completed.

Also, as ridiculous as it may sound, you want to make sure that the owner is, in fact, moving. Otherwise, you might be stuck with a long, sticky, expensive, and emotionally draining eviction proceeding.

If you notice anything wrong with the house during your final walk-through, tell your real estate agent. Do not approach the seller yourself. If you find the home in less than decent condition, you're very likely to get royally ticked off. The owner is likely to be peeved at your complaints. In this situation, it is truly best to employ the services of a middleman; that is, your agent.

Here's a checklist for your walk-through:

- *Are all major systems operational?* Flip every switch. Turn on the air-conditioning, the heat, and every major appliance. Run the showers and all the faucets. Flush the toilets.

- *Is everything you bought still there?* If you paid good money for the curtains, make sure they still hang on their rods. If you're shelling out a few extra bucks for a washer and dryer, check that they still sit in their nook.

And make sure there's not a big, empty indentation in the backyard where your aboveground pool or spa is supposed to sit.

- *Has the junk been removed?* If your contract stipulates that the current owners take with them the unused freezer in the basement or the rusted-out swing set in the backyard, make sure they're gone.

- *Is the seller ready to move out?* Taking a final walk-through a day or two before the closing, this is what you don't want to see: A homey scene, the books still lined up straight in their cases in the living room, the kitchen neat as a pin and well stocked, clothes still hanging in the closet, and so on. Clearly, no one can pack up years' worth of stuff in a day or two, so if your sellers haven't by now made a huge dent in their packing chores, you may have a problem. Talk to your real estate agent. Let him or her get the scoop on whether the current owners actually plan to, um, move. If they are being held up for some reason, you can either push back the closing date or charge them a very, very high daily rent to continue to use the property for a few days after closing.

- *If you're buying a newly built home . . .* Again, check all the major systems and appliances. Bring along a small appliance (clock, radio, or hair dryer, for example) and plug it into each outlet. Make sure they all work. Also check to see that the landscaping is done, the doorbells and garage door openers are installed, all the windows and screens are in place, and so on.

If during your walk-through you've detected substantial problems, you might want to arrange for yet another tour, this one slated for about five minutes before you actually close on the property. If the owners have rectified the problems, terrific. If they have not, politely demand that some of the purchase price be held in escrow until they do.

Planning for the Move

We've talked a bit about what you have to do to buy your new house. Now let's discuss leaving your old digs and preparing yourself for the move.

Dealing with Landlords

As you read this, you're probably still renting an apartment or house. Maybe you were lucky enough to schedule the closing so that it coincides with the last (or near to last) day of your lease. Maybe. But, more likely, you're going to have to sit down and talk with your landlord about either breaking your current lease or staying on in your apartment for an extra few weeks after your lease has expired.

If you need to break a lease, hope for a reasonable landlord. If you're lucky enough to have one, and if you have proven yourself a good tenant, that landlord may willingly release you from your contract. You might even get your security deposit back. The trick here is to give the landlord plenty of notice that you're planning to move. This allows the landlord enough time to find a new tenant. If your landlord says, "Tough luck. You have nine months left on your lease and you're gonna have to keep paying the rent for that time," you may want to speak with a lawyer to see what your rights are in your state.

But what if your lease ends on December 31st and your closing is scheduled for January 15th? Again, you need to ask your landlord if you can continue to rent your apartment, on a day-to-day basis, for an extra several weeks. Remember, your closing may be delayed (see "The Delay Game" on page 131). So, for safety's sake, see if you can keep your rental for at least a week after the initial closing date. Sure, you might end up paying an extra week's rent (or an entire month's rent if a week's extension isn't allowed) for nothing. But that's easier than finding storage space for your stuff and checking into a hotel if your closing should be delayed.

Also consider this: Once you've moved into your new home, will you have to paint, clean, perform minor repairs, lay new carpets, and so forth? Even though you're strapped for cash, it might be worth it to continue renting your apartment for a week or two (or a month, as the case may be) after the closing. This gives you the chance to make these small but necessary renovations without having to worry about spilling paint thinner all over your $2,000 computer.

Again, if your landlord refuses to let you stay on past the term of your lease, you should arrange temporary housing for yourself and temporary storage for your stuff several weeks before closing. Also, because many hotels don't allow pets, you'll prob-

ably have to make arrangements to board Rover or Kitty in a kennel or with friends.

Time Out, Please

Have some vacation time coming? You may want to consider taking a few days off when you move. You're probably planning to relocate on a weekend but sometimes a weekend just won't cut it. The excitement of closing, combined with the hassle of moving, will exhaust you. You may need a few days simply to recoup and unpack. Consider taking some vacation time. Talk to your employer as early as possible to schedule this.

TAX BREAKS FOR MOVING

In some instances, you can deduct moving expenses from your federal income taxes. You're allowed to do this when your move is job related (new position, transfer, etc.) and you are forced to move a certain number of miles from your current home. Talk with an accountant for the details.

The Move Itself

You should start getting quotes from moving companies as far in advance of the closing as you can. (See the sidebar on page 126 for tips on how to hire a good mover.) If you plan a do-it-yourself relocation—getting by, as the Beatles said, with a little help from your friends—start calling around as soon as possible to see who is willing and able to help you on moving day. Remember, your friends have lives. They may want to assist you, but they'll also want to know on exactly what date that assistance is expected.

Want to Live in the Dark?

Two weeks before moving/closing, call all the utility companies servicing your new neighborhood. Give them projected start dates for:

• Phone

• Electricity

• Gas

Choosing the Right Mover

It seems that exposé after exposé has recently detailed moving horror stories, usually centered on the shabby—and sometimes illegal—practices employed by so-called "professional movers."

You should take some time to find a reputable mover because you don't want to get trapped in a web of missing, broken, or nondelivered possessions; surprise fees sprung on you by the movers before they agree to unload your stuff; and lawsuits. A little research now will save you from a lot of hassles later.

First, either go with a name your recognize or with a company that comes with the recommendation of your friends and relatives.

Second, call the Better Business Bureau to see if any complaints have been lodged against the movers you are considering.

Third, make sure to get the physical address of any moving company you interview. Then go visit the address. Does it feel to you like a professional organization? Or does it look like "Joe's Fly-by-Nite Inc."? Trust your gut.

Fourth, sign a contract outlining exactly what the mover will charge for services. The moving company may quote you a price of $1,000 to move, say, your furniture plus 30 boxes. Don't be surprised if the price rises on moving day, when you discover you actually have 45 boxes. But the price should contractually rise in proportion to your original deal. If the mover agreed to move 30 boxes for $1,000, clearly, you should not pay $3,000 for the company to move 45 boxes.

Finally, some very reputable movers offer prices considerably lower than other very reputable movers. Call around to get quotes or check out the Relocation Wizard at http://www.homefair.com for rates.

- Trash

- Cable

- Water, if necessary

Your real estate agent should have a list of their phone numbers. If your closing should be pushed back, another round of telephone calls will postpone start-up dates for these services.

What to Bring to the Closing

All you really have to bring to the closing is yourself, your aspirations, your hopes, and your dreams for a good life in your new home. If only the universe operated that way. This is what you *really* have to bring to the closing:

- Proof that you have fulfilled all the requirements demanded by your lender in its letter of commitment to you. This proof includes receipts for insurance policies bought, for example.

- Loads of money. Remember, you cannot settle your down payment and closing costs with a personal check. Personal checks simply are not accepted at closing. You'll need to use a cashier's check, certified check, or wire transfer. Or, of course, cash.

You may wonder how you'll know exactly how much to make out the cashier's check for. Don't worry. Your lender will tally up the figures for you in a closing statement and mail the statement to you or your agent a few days before closing. This statement will outline exactly what is being charged by whom and will indicate which party (buyer or seller) has agreed to pay which charges.

Following is a list of what you can expect to have to bring with you on closing day. Remember, though, your commitment letter and settlement statement should be your ultimate guides.

- Closing statement

- Commitment letter from the lender

- Receipt of payment for one year's worth of homeowners insurance

- Receipt of payment for mortgage insurance, if such insurance is required by the lender

- Receipt of payment for title insurance, if you were told to buy this protection before closing day

What You Will Have to Do or Buy at Closing

Closing is the moment of truth and, before you actually sign the papers, you need to ensure that all eventualities have been accounted for. Like a wedding ceremony, it's a matter of speaking now or forever holding your peace.

Remember the $2,000 roof job that the sellers promised to have completed before closing day? If your walk-through indicates recent signs of leakage, don't take the sellers' word for it when they say, "Oh, the roofer has been so busy, but he promises to come by two weeks from Thursday. We'll meet him at the house and cut a check to pay him then."

Maybe you have moral sellers who truly do plan to meet with and pay the roofer two weeks after closing. But don't bet on it. You should either postpone closing, or insist that part of the purchase price be held in escrow until the job is completed.

Or suppose the sellers, at closing, say they've gotten backed up and just need "a few more days" to actually move out of the house? There are two schools of thought. One says that you go ahead with the closing, charging the sellers an exorbitant "daily rent." The rent should be so high that the current owners have a real incentive to move quickly. But suppose they live there for a week or two, refuse to pay you the rent, and worse, refuse to move out. Do you really want to get stuck with a costly eviction proceeding? A second, and perhaps surer, school of thought states that you should delay closing until the sellers are out of the house.

Over the course of the closing, you will review and sign loan documents. Other documents—such as the deed, bill of sale, and title—will be exchanged between the title agent, seller, and you. Then you pay up.

You can expect to pay your down payment, minus any earnest money you have already delivered. And there are, of course, the closing costs. As discussed earlier in this chapter, "closing costs" is a catch phrase covering all the charges—from lawyer's fees to points—associated with transferring and are typically paid on the big day. In a worst-case scenario, you, as the buyer, might be expected to pay for them all. But the savvy homebuyer, employing some of the negotiating tools discussed in chapter 6, may have convinced the seller to shoulder at least part of the closing cost load.

Here's a list of some of those costs:

- *Points.* A point is a monetary unit equivalent to 1 percent of the mortgage loan amount. For example, if you have borrowed $40,000, each point is worth $400. As a general rule of thumb, the interest you pay on the mortgage loan decreases slightly with each point you are willing to pay up front.

- *Prorated interest for the rest of the month.* Your lender will prorate the monthly interest on your mortgage to a daily amount. You will have to prepay the interest for the month you move in, calculated from the day of the closing. For example, if you close on June 15th, you will have to pay 16 days of interest, covering the 15th through the 30th. If you close on December 15th, you will have to pay 17 days of interest, covering the 15th through the 31st. Depending on the amount of cash you have on hand, you may want to schedule your closing for the end of the month. This scenario contains some good news, though. You are used to paying rent. Rent is paid in advance, meaning you pay your landlord on July 1st for the privilege of living in your unit through the end of the month. Mortgage payments, however, are made in arrears. If your mortgage payment is made July 1st, you are actually, at that time, paying your lender for having lived in your house through June. So, while you have to pay prorated interest for the first month you move in, you get to skip your

mortgage payment the next month. Normal mortgage payments resume the second full month you're living in the house.

- *Title insurance.* Your lender will demand title insurance, even though someone (usually the seller) has paid for a title search. This insurance protects the lender, and the lender only, against unforeseen claims of ownership to the property. Here's an example. Suppose you have just purchased a home that has been in the same family for generations. Your title company may have missed a claim by the seller's third cousin Henry twice removed. Your bank asks that you pay for title insurance for such an eventuality. Title insurance is usually paid in a single premium. Remember, however, the protection your bank mandates covers its interests only. You may want to purchase additional insurance to cover your growing financial stake in the property; that is, your down payment and future mortgage payments.

- *Loan origination fee.* There's no easy way to say this. This is basically a fee that the bank charges you for the privilege of securing a loan. You may think that you are already paying the institution an awful lot of money in interest for your loan privileges, and you'd be right. But the bank may charge you this fee as well—mostly because it can.

- *Assumption fee.* If you've assumed the mortgage from the seller, the bank may charge you for the privilege.

- *Additional months of homeowners insurance.* Although you've already paid for a year's worth of homeowners insurance up front, your lending institution may ask for a few more months' worth. (The lender will prorate the policy to calculate your monthly premium.)

- *Several months of property taxes.* The bank will prorate your projected yearly property taxes, and ask for at least a few months' worth up front. This money will be kept in an escrow account.

- *Fees for settlement of title.* These usually run less than $400.

- *Lawyer's fees, if an attorney was involved in the sale.*

- *Recording fees.* This is the cost of recording your deed with the county government. It usually runs less than $100.

- *Condo, co-op, or homeowners association fees.* Some such organizations charge move-in fees.

The Delay Game

The entire closing will likely take less than two hours. Many even take less than an hour. That, of course, assumes everyone's ducks are in a row.

But problems do often arise, delaying the closing for a few hours or a few days. Here are some of the most common problems and how you can handle them.

- *The figures don't add up.* Suppose, because of information provided to you from the lender, you believe your down payment and closing costs total $15,779. When the math is checked at closing, you realize that it's actually $16,001. Because the title agent won't accept a personal check, you may have to run across town to your bank get yet another cashier's check. You can often avoid this sort of delay by bringing a few hundred dollars in cash with you to the closing.

- *You spotted problems during your walk-through that have yet to be fixed.* If the problems were structural, you can either wait to close until they have been fixed or insist that part of your payment be held in escrow until they are corrected. Only then can the money be released to the seller.

- *The title search revealed an unexpected claim against the property.* Under no circumstances should you close on the house until its current owners have settled the claim.

- *The sellers ain't movin'.* This often happens when the sellers own deal has fallen through—for example, they thought they were buying another home but they couldn't get a mortgage, or their sellers have reneged. As discussed above, you have two choices. You can either close with a legal deal demanding a high daily, weekly, or monthly rent from the sellers

until they move out; or, safer yet, you can postpone closing until the sellers are out of the house.

- *The house blew up.* John Irving fans might remember a wonderful scene in the movie version of *The World According to Garp.* Garp and his wife are looking at a house and readying themselves for an offer. Then an airplane crashes into the second story. "We'll take it!" Garp exclaims to the astonished real estate agent. When his wife protests, he says, "But honey, it's been disaster-proofed!"

While the Garp scenario is unlikely, houses sometimes do suffer damage from disasters such as fires, floods, and earthquakes after a seller has accepted an offer, but before the close. Your contract no doubt contains an "out clause" for just such an incident.

Obviously, the price of the house gets renegotiated (or the deal disappears) if the house (or part of it) is no longer actually standing. So if you find yourself up this creek, talk to a qualified attorney.

Top Five Things to Do Right Now

1. Buy homeowners insurance and any other items demanded by your lender's letter of commitment.

2. Talk to your landlord about breaking your lease or staying on for a few weeks after your lease has expired. If you cannot stay on until closing, arrange temporary housing for yourself and your pets and storage for your possessions.

3. Decide whether you will hire professional movers or move your possessions yourself. If you go the professional route, begin to call for rates. If you're doing it yourself, call friends and family for help.

4. Call the utility companies serving your new neighborhood, and give them a turn-on date.

5. Schedule a final walk-through of your new home.

Don't Forget to Get . . .

What do you expect to get at closing? Before you say, "A house, stupid," think of all the things you need to actually unlock your house. That's right, folks. In the flurry of passing deeds and checks, more than one new homeowner has forgotten to make sure that the seller delivers:

- Keys to every lock on the property, including those on toolsheds, outbuildings, and so on

- Combinations to any security alarms (remember to change the combinations when you move in)

- User guides for appliances and other manuals

- Mail box keys

- Garage door openers

Settling IN

CHAPTER NINE

You've scouted the neighborhoods, found the house, secured financing, dealt with the nearly inevitable closing delays, hired the right mover and now, a little nervous and excited, you fumble with the keys and unlock the door to your first home.

You look around. Maybe there's just some touch-up painting to do, or maybe you're facing a few weeks worth of hard-core home improvement. Still, you breathe a sigh of relief. You just bought a home!

And you're right. You've made your way through the homebuying part of your adventure.

In this chapter, though, you'll learn a little bit about "home owning." This, too, is a new experience for you. You'll have to deal with the twin urges to splurge on your new home and, perhaps suffering some buyers remorse over the monthly mortgage payments, trying to pinch your pennies until they scream. You'll also have to cope with the unwanted telephone solicitations mounted by salespeople who target new

homeowners. Maybe you'll also encounter unexpected defects in the home or learn to live with neighbors who prove to be not exactly your type.

Home ownership is rife with small joys and unexpected frustrations. You'll welcome the joys. Here are some hints on dealing with the frustrations.

Money Matters

Money issues will weigh heavily on your mind in the coming months. You may start to panic over large monthly mortgage payments and become so tight with a buck that your friends start whispering "Scrooge" behind your back. Conversely, a psychological desire to turn your home into a showplace may lead you to throw financial caution to the wind in the quest for the right sofa.

Don't allow yourself to fall into either of these traps. Instead, take a slow but sure financial path that includes rebuilding the savings your down payment may have depleted.

The Decorating Pit

This home is yours, and you naturally take pride in ownership. But too many new homeowners want their digs to metamorphose, instantly, into showplaces. While the house may stand prettily on its own (after a good scrubbing or a coat of paint), all of a sudden your furniture looks a little shabby. A few new sofas might do nicely—preferably, a Louis XIV. And you'd really, really like to replace that old, apartment trod-upon rag rug with a new Aubusson. Certainly, some Waterford crystal should replace your old jelly glasses. And you bought the house, in part, because its backyard is large enough to contain a pool. Why not put one in now?

Resist these temptations. Many, many new homeowners, temporarily "cash poor," have taken to building up crushing credit card debts for home decor and renovations. Don't become one of them. Spend wisely on your new home and put off your decorating dreams until you have the money to pay for them.

"I'm Not Spending Another Penny, Ever" or "What Did We Do?"

For every new homeowner willing to go into credit card debt to decorate his new place, there are others who, 10 minutes after closing on the house, are hit by such panic that they consider putting it up for sale immediately. This is called *buyer's remorse,* a psychological phenomenon that attacks some people after a major purchase.

It happens like this. After the adrenaline of closing, you sit down and take a minute to think. You suddenly realize that you're tied to this purchase—the largest you've ever made—for the length of the mortgage, usually 30 years. At this point, you can think of nothing but this seemingly monstrous debt. You may even begin to hyperventilate.

Calm down. These can be scary feelings. But sometimes just knowing these feelings have a name—buyer's remorse—can help you combat them. So can reminding yourself of the following:

- *Just how poor are you?* Remember, you may make up for those big monthly mortgage payments when tax season comes and you begin deducting interest from your federal income tax.

- *You're not wasting money renting.* You are investing in your future by building equity in a home. In addition, your home may appreciate as time passes. If that happens, you'll garner a tidy profit when it comes time to sell.

- *Hey, the bank liked you.* You might now be fretting about your income and earning potential but the lender liked you enough to actually loan you some money. No banker is going to say, "There's no way that Susie and Harry can keep up with their monthly mortgage payments, but they seem like such nice folks that I thought I'd just give them the loan anyway." Banks are in the business of making money through investments and interest payments—not by foreclosing on homes. If your self-confidence is at an all-time low, you might, for a bit, want to trust the bank's view of you rather than your own.

Saving for a Rainy Day

Once you've moved into your new home and given yourself a little time to catch your breath, you might want to think about how you can replenish the savings account you so recently depleted. You may feel that you don't have to worry about this too much because you enjoy a very secure job. But don't kid yourself. Many, many secure jobs have gone by the wayside through no fault at all of the employees who held them. A general rule of thumb is that you should have on hand enough cash to get you through three to six months of unemployment.

To both meet the mortgage and replenish your savings account, you may have to devise some cost-cutting measures. You can probably think of several off the top of your head. Cut the number of nights on the town from two to one each week. Go without cable TV. Make do with fans rather than air-conditioning. Buy inexpensive generic items at the grocery store rather than their brand-name counterparts. Mow your own lawn rather than hiring a landscaper. Go through your budget and try to identify ten regular expenditures you can cut or reduce. Then do it.

There are also ways that you can save money on home ownership itself. Following are some good ones:

Cutting Insurance Costs

Reconsider your homeowners insurance policy. As discussed in chapter 8, your lender no doubt mandated that you secure homeowners insurance before closing. The insurance consisted of both casualty—covering loss of property due to fire, weather, vandalism, theft, robbery, and so on—and liability—in case your great aunt Agnes should slip and fall on your property. If your premiums now seem a little high to you, here are some ways to cut insurance costs while still maintaining the coverage you need.

- *Consider a higher deductible.* Your insurance premiums dip in inverse proportion to the deductible you select. (The lower the deductible, the higher the premium.) However, because you certainly don't plan on getting robbed every year or so, and because tornadoes are unlikely to bang your

door down on alternate weekends, you may want to consider upping your deductible. Depending on rates in your area, you may find that lower premiums more than make up for having to shell out a few extra "deductible" bucks in case an emergency arises.

- *Bundle your policies.* Insurance companies are often willing to give you a break on premiums if you have more than one policy with the same company. So consider buying your home and car policies from the same corporation. If you're self-employed, you may also want to consider buying your home, car, health, disability, and life insurance policies from the same insurer.

- *Shop around.* Insurance firms sometimes seem to operate a little like the airlines: costs for the same services vary widely from outfit to outfit. Call around to make sure you're getting the best rate. And if you're not, call your carrier and let them know you've found a better rate and give them a chance to meet it. If they don't, move on to the greener pastures.

- *Be safe.* Smoke alarms, fire alarms, and burglar alarms not only protect you and your family, they can also help you earn lower insurance rates.

For more information, check out the Consumers Independent Guide to Homeowners Insurance at http://www.iiaa.com/consumer/homeguid.htm/.

Wasting Energy

You know to turn the lights off when you go to sleep at night. You know to replace a washer if your kitchen faucet starts dripping. But while focusing on the trees, you may be missing the great big forest.

Consider the insulation in your home. Proper insulation will help keep you cozy in the winter, cooler in the summer. Lower electric bills will mean that you will easily, over time, recoup the cost of its installation. Also, you need to check to see if your heating/cooling systems are running poorly, or leaking, or otherwise gobbling up the dollars. Check them out as soon as possible.

Most local energy companies will provide free or low-cost energy efficiency inspections of your home. These inspections almost always turn up easily fixable energy inefficiencies that are costing you money. Call your local electric or gas company for details on setting up an inspection.

If the Value of Your Home Falls

A sentence no homeowner wants to hear: You can save money if the value of your home falls. Homeowners will only pick up the words "value of your home falls" and immediately start to panic.

Take heart, though: Even the soundest neighborhoods go through property value ebbs and flows. You may correctly choose to hang tough through an ebb. And you can save money by alerting your county property appraiser's office to the fact that your home is, for the moment, apparently not worth what you paid for it.

Let's say that you bought a house for $120,000. Your property taxes are based on a home worth $120,000 in the open market. But, over the last several months, houses in your neighborhood have sold for $115,000. That means that the actual value of your home, at this particular moment, is likely to be a little less than what you originally spent for it.

Your property assessor is unlikely to adjust your assessment downward, however, unless you tell that official about your problems. But you should not continue to pay property taxes on a $120,000 house when, in fact, your home may be worth only $115,000.

File a challenge in your property tax assessor's office (usually located in your county courthouse). The clerks there can explain to you the exact procedures but, in general, you are expected to prove your case.

To show that local property values have fallen, develop a list of homes that have sold in your neighborhood in the last six months to a year and note what they sold for. Your real estate agent should be both able and willing to help you with this. If not, you can put together a list through information on file in your property assessor's office.

Refinancing: The Big "Should I"

As interest rates fall and rise and fall, every homeowner carrying a mortgage faces the question, "Should I refinance?" The answer is a resounding "It depends." Here's a step-by-step guide to help you decide whether or not refinancing is a good move.

- *Wait until interest rates drop at least one full point.* Because of the up-front fees you have to pay for refinancing, trying to get a new mortgage when interest rates have dropped one-tenth of 1 percent makes absolutely no financial sense. The fees would eat up any savings. You can track interest rates through regular news reports or in the business section of your local newspaper.

- *Contact banks and other lending institutions that refinance mortgages.* The key word here is *contact,* not sign on with. Talk to a representative. The rep will likely break the figures down into the amount the institution can save you, each month, in mortgage payments. As an aside, he or she will tell you that loan fees and title insurance will cost you another chunk of change. For example, say that the lender's rep has told you that you can save $200 in mortgage payments each month but that you will have to pay $5,000 in refinancing fees.

- *Learn how much you're really saving.* Remember, you can deduct mortgage payments from your federal income taxes. Let's say that you are saving $200 in mortgage payments each month and you are in the 28 percent tax bracket. That means that, once tax breaks are taken into account, you really only save $144 each month ($200 x .28 = $56; $200 − $56 = $144).

- *Determine how long it will take to recoup your refinancing fees.* For the sake of argument, we've projected refinancing fees of $5,000, versus your actual, realized savings of $144 each month. You would have to live in your current home for 35 months to simply recoup these financing fees.

- *Decide how long you plan to live in the house.* If you are a happily single poet who has just gotten the deal of the century on a dollhouse in Key West, you may reply "I plan to live here forever." Then refinancing, in the sce-

Refinancing Worksheet

This worksheet is designed to help you determine how long it will take for the lower monthly payments you would enjoy by refinancing to offset the cost of taking out the new loan. Costs for the items below can vary widely, but we have used typical amounts for a $100,000 loan in the example.

Your Refinancing Costs

Item	Example	Your Loan
1. Points	$2,000	$ _____
2. Application fee	100	_____
3. Title search and insurance	500	_____
4. Inspections	250	_____
5. Lender's underwriting fee	250	_____
6. Document preparation fee	200	_____
7. Credit report	50	_____
8. Appraisal	250	_____
9. Attorney or escrow fees	500	_____
10. Recording fees	50	_____
11. Other fees	150	_____
12. Your Total Refinancing Costs	$4,300	$ _____

Your Payback

	Example	Your Loan
1. Current monthly payment (based on 30-year loan at 10%)	$878	$ _____
2. Subtract new monthly payment after refinancing is complete (based on 30-year loan at 8%)	− 734	− _____
3. Monthly savings from refinancing	= 144	= _____
4. Divide monthly savings ($144) into total cost of refinancing ($4,300)	29.8	
NUMBER OF MONTHS NEEDED TO RECOUP REFINANCING COSTS:	30	_____

nario outlined above, would be well worth it for you. If, however, you are a married couple living in that same dollhouse for an investment and plan to move when you get pregnant, with any luck, in a year or so, you'll save money by *not* refinancing.

Save Money by Not Buying Stupid Stuff or "Why Do These People Keep Calling Me?"

Once you take possession of your new home, you'll get unsolicited telephone calls from salespeople offering everything from a new roof to new carpeting to insurance. If you're like a lot of new homeowners, you will be amazed by the sheer frequency of these telephone calls. You will start to wonder, "Why are all these people calling me?" Here's why.

Your purchase (lot, improvements, and price) was, by law, recorded in your county courthouse. Many local newspapers also print this info. Savvy salespeople, when prospecting for new clients, turn to this readily available information. You've just turned into a magnet for every salesperson on the block.

You can easily deal with several of these offers. Suppose you've bought a ten-year-old house and you receive a solicitation for a new roof. You know, from your home inspection report, that the roof was made to last and it should have no problems in the near future. Even if it does, you have a home warranty to cover it. You feel safe with a polite "no." Or let's say someone calls you regarding new carpeting. You know that the carpeting in your home is beginning to look a little threadbare but you've decided that, because of financial considerations, replacement will simply have to wait for a year. You would feel comfortable refusing this salesperson's pitch.

Some pitches, however, will likely hit your recent feelings of money vulnerability. These include offers of mortgage insurance that would take care of payments in the event of your disability or death. Although you would certainly want to provide for your family in case of disability or death, these insurance policies, in general, are not a good idea. (Remember, this mortgage insurance is quite different from the insurance you bought before closing to protect the bank in case you renege on your payments.)

First, mortgage insurance policies offer too-small payouts for too-large premiums. Second, you may, either independently or through your employer, already have disability and/or life insurance. If you feel underinsured, shop around for your own life/disability policies. Don't just accept the first offer that comes to you via an unsolicited telephone call.

If Something Goes Wrong

You hope that life in your new home will be a bed of roses. That's every homeowner's dream. However, problems do sometimes arise—concerning everything from undisclosed defects in the home to not-so-nice neighbors living next door.

Here's how you can cope with some of these problems.

Undisclosed Defects in the House

You had a home inspection performed and you carefully read the sellers disclosure. Still, to your consternation, after moving in you find a previously undiscovered or unreported defect.

If you think that the sellers are automatically required to fix the problem for you because they failed to note it on the seller's disclosure, think again. Sellers' disclosures are funny things. The law requires that sellers list defects that they "know or should have known" about. That's a fairly vague standard. Should the sellers necessarily have known about the short in the eighth outlet on the left wall of their semifinished basement? Only a lawyer can tell you for sure.

If you're faced with this type of situation and have no home warranty, you should call your real estate agent and ask for the sellers' new telephone number. Then call up the sellers, express your concerns, and hope that they are ethical—that they will put the problem right, at their expense.

And maybe they will. But you have no guarantee. They may say, "You bought it. The amenities are yours to enjoy, and the problems are now your responsibility. Good luck." Your only option at this point is a lawsuit. And you don't really want that.

This is why, as mentioned in chapter 8, home warranties prove so crucial. You know all about warranties. You can't swing a dead cat in an electronics store these days without hitting a warranteed product. Your computer. Your large-screen TV. Your dishwasher.

They all come with either store or manufacturers' warranties that, basically, state "If something goes wrong with this product within a certain period of time, we'll either repair or replace it for you for free. " Home warranties are no different.

Home warranties are usually paid for by the seller, as part of your contract to buy. Insist that the seller pay for this coverage. It usually costs less than $400. You can ask your real estate agent for some brochures to figure out which warranty suits your fancy. Coverage varies from warranty to warranty but they can be written to cover:

- Built-in appliances

- Home structure

- Roof

- Plumbing

- Electrical

- Pools and spas

Nasty Neighbors

You've already learned about the importance of surveying or "scoping out" a neighborhood before you move in. Still, unexpected problems can arise. A single inappropriate household can mar the atmosphere of an otherwise pleasant neighborhood.

Suppose that existing neighbors, or people who move into town after you do, prove to be members of the "Let's let our three vicious rottweilers stroll through the neighborhood, pooping on everyone's front lawn and attacking pedestrians" community; or the "Let's paint our home sea green with purple shutters" community; or the "Let's play our CDs full blast until four in the morning" community; or the "We

don't believe in tending to our front lawn so we've decided to let the grass grow naturally to the point where it obscures our front door" community. What to do?

First, you need to talk to your neighbors. People can't read minds, you know. They need to hear in plain English what the problem is. And you may be surprised by their response.

A neighbor might say, "You know, we felt so bad for the rottweiler puppies. They'd been abandoned by the side of the road and we trained them as well as we could. We put a fence up in our backyard but they keep jumping over it." Here's where you explain how you or your best friend or your cousin had a similar experience and how the local Humane Society offers some very-low-cost obedience training.

Or "Gosh. The house you bought was vacant for so long, we'd sort of forgotten that our music would bother anybody. We're sorry."

Or "I'm so sorry about the grass but my husband keeled over last month and I have a heart murmur. I can't cut it myself but right now I don't have enough money to pay someone to cut it for me." You might suggest the widow contact local social service agencies who provide low- to no-cost homeowner services or organize a group of neighborhood kids to tend the lawn.

Of course, any or all of the above neighbors may also say, "Get the heck off my property." If this happens, don't despair. You have recourse.

If you live in a deed-restricted community, condo, or co-op you may want to go to the homeowners association to lodge a complaint against a possible breaking of the bylaws. This is, after all, one of the reasons you may have opted for a condo or co-op—a homeowners association that will handle the issues affecting the members' best interests. And it's part of what your communal fees are paying for.

If you live in an historic district, home care issues may be enforced by your local planning board.

If you live in a regular, old-fashioned neighborhood, you can, as a last resort, report the loud CD-playing couple to the police for breaking the peace; you can call animal

Becoming Part of Your Community

Depending on how far your new home sits from your old place, you may, upon moving, face the challenge of making new friends or otherwise breaking into your community.

You may be counting on your new neighbors to become your friends, and often this will happen. But suppose you and your neighbors have interests too widely different to truly become friends? Or suppose they already have so many friends that they're not terribly interested in new buddies?

Fear not. There are still many ways that you can become a part of your community.

Check out local fraternal and social organizations. Many local libraries maintain lists of the social clubs operating within a city's borders and many municipalities post similar listings on their Web sites. If you live in a burgeoning area, newcomers clubs can provide you with a rich vein of people who, like you, are eager to make new friends.

Second, consider volunteering for an organization that stirs your passions. A few hours each week spent helping out at the local animal shelter will not only provide some much needed help to a worthwhile organization but will also likely win you some new friends in the process.

Volunteer for local cleanup or beautification projects, political campaigns, school activities. Everywhere you turn, there's a group that'd be grateful for your help and that's teeming with people who share your interests. So get out there and lend a hand.

control about the free-range rottweilers; and you can contact the local planning department about unkempt front lawns.

Clearly, these are last-ditch efforts. Remember, even if police or governmental bodies talk some sense into your neighbors, you—not they—have to live next to these folks. Your calling the cops will do little to promote harmonious neighborhood relations, so make sure you exhaust every other option first.

Remodel or Move?

If you're like many Americans, your housing needs will change over time. Within a few years you may need to decide whether to remodel/expand your current home or simply buy a new one. No matter how much you like your house, you have some hard decisions to make before you decide to remodel it.

First, think of why you want to remodel. If you adore your house, have made terrific friends in the neighborhood, and hope to stay put forever (or at least for the foreseeable future) you may want to consider remodeling.

Don't consider remodeling as a moneymaking move, however. Studies show that remodeling expenses are rarely recouped when it comes time to sell the home. The exception to this is kitchen improvements. So, if you really want to stay in your current house but want to install a pool in the backyard, by all means do so. Enjoy your pool but don't think that you'll recoup the $12,000 construction costs when it comes time to sell. Conversely, if you want a house with a pool and have grown out of or grown tired of your current dwelling, you may want to consider a move.

Here are some other things to consider when trying to decide whether remodeling or moving is right for you.

- *Will your planning/zoning board let you do what you want to do?* The construction of a new bedroom or bathroom may violate your planning board's setback rules (laws governing the number of feet a home sits back from the street or sidewalk). The office you want to build onto the side of your house may violate local zoning laws, especially if working out of your home will bring a steady stream of cars into an otherwise residential

neighborhood. A homeowners association may have similar rules for those living in its deed-restricted development.

- *What is the status of property values in your neighborhood?* If home values in your neighborhood seem to be stable or increasing and you think that the value of your home is increasing the longer you stay there, you might want to consider remodeling to make a pleasant space for yourself until your property prices peak. However, if you believe that property values are on the downswing, you may want to consider moving.

- *Is remodeling cost effective?* Suppose that a reputable contractor could add two rooms to your house—a bedroom and a den—for about $45,000. But what if you could buy the size house you need, in a better neighborhood, for the sale price of your house plus an additional $35,000? Again, you might want to consider moving.

For more information, check out the National Association of the Remodeling Industry Web site at http://www.nari/org. In addition to giving you design ideas and teaching you how to identify a good contractor from a bad one, it can also link you to NARI approved remodelers working in your area.

And in the End . . .

Reading though this book, you've learned that home buying isn't a smooth and easy process. There may be a few glitches with home ownership, as well. But home ownership is a sound choice for those who want to build equity in a property, rather than just throwing their money away on rent month after month. In addition, as housing prices rise, you may realize a tidy little profit when it comes time to sell.

Perhaps more important, the dream of home ownership is strongly ingrained in the American psyche. Something you own just seems more cozy, more homey, more yours than any rental ever will.

Top Five Things to Do Right Now

1. Go introduce yourself to your neighbors and start paving the way for sound neighborhood relations during your tenure in your new home.

2. Sit down and reassess your household budget, cutting where necessary.

3. Begin to rebuild your savings.

4. Call your local energy company for an energy efficiency inspection of your home.

5. Contact your local property assessor to make sure that your home is assessed at its correct value. If the assessment is too high, challenge it. If the assessment is too low, well, let your conscience be your guide.

APPENDIX

Monthly Payment Tables

Your monthly mortgage payment will include interest on the amount borrowed, plus a bit more intended to whittle down the principal still owed. As the loan is gradually paid, less interest is owed, and a larger portion of each payment can go toward principal.

The following tables cover loan terms of 1 to 40 years, with interest rates between 2 percent and 19 percent.

To find your mortgage payment:

1. Search the left-hand column until you find the interest rate on your loan.
2. Search the top line for the number of years you will be making payments.
3. Follow the percentage line across and the "number of years" column down until the two intersect. The figure indicated is the monthly dollar amount necessary to amortize (pay off) a loan of $1,000 in the given time, at the given rate of interest.
   Example: If a 10 percent loan has a term of 25 years, the two lines intersect at 9.0870. This means that $9.087 a month, for 25 years, would pay off a loan of $1,000 at 10 percent interest.
4. Multiply the figure indicated by the number of thousands being borrowed. This gives you the monthly payment necessary to amortize the entire loan.
   Example: If, in the example given with step 3, the loan amount is $74,500, this represents 74.5 thousands. Multiplying $9.087 by 74.5 gives you $676.9816, which would be rounded off to a monthly payment of $676.98.

The figure you have found represents principal and interest only; if a lending institution requires escrow for taxes and insurance, one-twelfth of those costs must be added to arrive at the PITI payment.

MONTHLY PAYMENT TO AMORTIZE A LOAN OF $1,000

Term of Loan

Interest Rate	1 Year	2 Years	3 Years	4 Years	5 Years	6 Years	7 Years	8 Years
2.000%	84.2389	42.5403	28.6426	21.6951	17.5278	14.7504	12.7674	11.2809
2.125%	84.2956	42.5952	28.6972	21.7497	17.5825	14.8054	12.8226	11.3364
2.250%	84.3524	42.6502	28.7518	21.8044	17.6373	14.8605	12.8780	11.3920
2.375%	84.4093	42.7053	28.8066	21.8592	17.6923	14.9157	12.9335	11.4478
2.500%	84.4661	42.7604	28.8614	21.9140	17.7474	14.9710	12.9892	11.5038
2.625%	84.5230	42.8155	28.9162	21.9690	17.8025	15.0265	13.0450	11.5600
2.750%	84.5799	42.8707	28.9712	22.0240	17.8578	15.0821	13.1009	11.6164
2.875%	84.6368	42.9259	29.0262	22.0791	17.9132	15.1378	13.1570	11.6729
3.000%	84.6937	42.9812	29.0812	22.1343	17.9687	15.1937	13.2133	11.7296
3.125%	84.7506	43.0365	29.1363	22.1896	18.0243	15.2497	13.2697	11.7864
3.250%	84.8076	43.0919	29.1915	22.2450	18.0800	15.3058	13.3263	11.8435
3.375%	84.8646	43.1473	29.2468	22.3005	18.1358	15.3620	13.3830	11.9007
3.500%	84.9216	43.2027	29.3021	22.3560	18.1917	15.4184	13.4399	11.9581
3.625%	84.9787	43.2582	29.3575	22.4116	18.2478	15.4749	13.4969	12.0156
3.750%	85.0357	43.3137	29.4129	22.4674	18.3039	15.5315	13.5540	12.0733
3.875%	85.0928	43.3693	29.4684	22.5232	18.3602	15.5883	13.6113	12.1312
4.000%	85.1499	43.4249	29.5240	22.5791	18.4165	15.6452	13.6688	12.1893
4.125%	85.2070	43.4806	29.5796	22.6350	18.4730	15.7022	13.7264	12.2475
4.250%	85.2642	43.5363	29.6353	22.6911	18.5296	15.7593	13.7842	12.3059
4.375%	85.3213	43.5920	29.6911	22.7472	18.5862	15.8166	13.8421	12.3645
4.500%	85.3785	43.6478	29.7469	22.8035	18.6430	15.8740	13.9002	12.4232
4.625%	85.4357	43.7036	29.8028	22.8598	18.6999	15.9316	13.9584	12.4822
4.750%	85.4930	43.7595	29.8588	22.9162	18.7569	15.9892	14.0167	12.5412
4.875%	85.5502	43.8154	29.9148	22.9727	18.8140	16.0470	14.0752	12.6005
5.000%	85.6075	43.8714	29.9709	23.0293	18.8712	16.1049	14.1339	12.6599
5.125%	85.6648	43.9274	30.0271	23.0860	18.9286	16.1630	14.1927	12.7195
5.250%	85.7221	43.9834	30.0833	23.1427	18.9860	16.2212	14.2517	12.7793
5.375%	85.7794	44.0395	30.1396	23.1996	19.0435	16.2795	14.3108	12.8392
5.500%	85.8368	44.0957	30.1959	23.2565	19.1012	16.3379	14.3700	12.8993
5.625%	85.8942	44.1518	30.2523	23.3135	19.1589	16.3964	14.4294	12.9596
5.750%	85.9516	44.2080	30.3088	23.3706	19.2168	16.4551	14.4890	13.0200
5.875%	86.0090	44.2643	30.3653	23.4278	19.2747	16.5139	14.5487	13.0807
6.000%	86.0664	44.3206	30.4219	23.4850	19.3328	16.5729	14.6086	13.1414
6.125%	86.1239	44.3770	30.4786	23.5424	19.3910	16.6320	14.6686	13.2024
6.250%	86.1814	44.4333	30.5353	23.5998	19.4493	16.6912	14.7287	13.2635
6.375%	86.2389	44.4898	30.5921	23.6573	19.5077	16.7505	14.7890	13.3248
6.500%	86.2964	44.5463	30.6490	23.7150	19.5661	16.8099	14.8494	13.3862
6.625%	86.3540	44.6028	30.7059	23.7726	19.6248	16.8695	14.9100	13.4479
6.750%	86.4115	44.6593	30.7629	23.8304	19.6835	16.9292	14.9708	13.5096
6.875%	86.4691	44.7159	30.8200	23.8883	19.7423	16.9890	15.0316	13.5716

MONTHLY PAYMENT TO AMORTIZE A LOAN OF $1,000

Term of Loan

Interest Rate	9 Years	10 Years	11 Years	12 Years	12 Years	14 Years	15 Years	16 Years
2.000%	10.1253	9.2013	8.4459	7.8168	7.2850	6.8295	6.4351	6.0903
2.125%	10.1811	9.2574	8.5023	7.8736	7.3420	6.8869	6.4928	6.1484
2.250%	10.2370	9.3137	8.5590	7.9305	7.3994	6.9446	6.5508	6.2068
2.375%	10.2932	9.3703	8.6158	7.9878	7.4570	7.0025	6.6092	6.2655
2.500%	10.3496	9.4270	8.6729	8.0453	7.5149	7.0608	6.6679	6.3246
2.625%	10.4061	9.4839	8.7303	8.1031	7.5730	7.1194	6.7269	6.3840
2.750%	10.4629	9.5411	8.7879	8.1611	7.6315	7.1783	6.7862	6.4438
2.875%	10.5198	9.5985	8.8457	8.2193	7.6902	7.2375	6.8459	6.5039
3.000%	10.5769	9.6561	8.9038	8.2779	7.7492	7.2970	6.9058	6.5643
3.125%	10.6343	9.7139	8.9621	8.3367	7.8085	7.3567	6.9661	6.6251
3.250%	10.6918	9.7719	9.0206	8.3957	7.8680	7.4168	7.0267	6.6862
3.375%	10.7495	9.8301	9.0793	8.4550	7.9279	7.4772	7.0876	6.7477
3.500%	10.8074	9.8886	9.1383	8.5145	7.9880	7.5378	7.1488	6.8095
3.625%	10.8655	9.9472	9.1976	8.5743	8.0484	7.5988	7.2104	6.8716
3.750%	10.9238	10.0061	9.2570	8.6344	8.1090	7.6601	7.2722	6.9340
3.875%	10.9823	10.0652	9.3167	8.6947	8.1700	7.7216	7.3344	6.9968
4.000%	11.0410	10.1245	9.3767	8.7553	8.2312	7.7835	7.3969	7.0600
4.125%	11.0998	10.1840	9.4368	8.8161	8.2926	7.8456	7.4597	7.1234
4.250%	11.1589	10.2438	9.4972	8.8772	8.3544	7.9080	7.5228	7.1872
4.375%	11.2181	10.3037	9.5579	8.9385	8.4164	7.9707	7.5862	7.2513
4.500%	11.2776	10.3638	9.6187	9.0001	8.4787	8.0338	7.6499	7.3158
4.625%	11.3372	10.4242	9.6798	9.0619	8.5413	8.0971	7.7140	7.3805
4.750%	11.3971	10.4848	9.7411	9.1240	8.6041	8.1607	7.7783	7.4456
4.875%	11.4571	10.5456	9.8027	9.1863	8.6672	8.2245	7.8430	7.5111
5.000%	11.5173	10.6066	9.8645	9.2489	8.7306	8.2887	7.9079	7.5768
5.125%	11.5777	10.6678	9.9265	9.3117	8.7942	8.3532	7.9732	7.6429
5.250%	11.6383	10.7292	9.9888	9.3748	8.8582	8.4179	8.0388	7.7093
5.375%	11.6990	10.7908	10.0512	9.4381	8.9223	8.4829	8.1047	7.7760
5.500%	11.7600	10.8526	10.1139	9.5017	8.9868	8.5483	8.1708	7.8430
5.625%	11.8212	10.9147	10.1769	9.5655	9.0515	8.6139	8.2373	7.9104
5.750%	11.8825	10.9769	10.2400	9.6296	9.1165	8.6797	8.3041	7.9781
5.875%	11.9440	11.0394	10.3034	9.6939	9.1817	8.7459	8.3712	8.0461
6.000%	12.0057	11.1021	10.3670	9.7585	9.2472	8.8124	8.4386	8.1144
6.125%	12.0677	11.1649	10.4309	9.8233	9.3130	8.8791	8.5062	8.1830
6.250%	12.1298	11.2280	10.4949	9.8884	9.3790	8.9461	8.5742	8.2519
6.375%	12.1920	11.2913	10.5592	9.9537	9.4453	9.0134	8.6425	8.3212
6.500%	12.2545	11.3548	10.6238	10.0192	9.5119	9.0810	8.7111	8.3908
6.625%	12.3172	11.4185	10.6885	10.0850	9.5787	9.1488	8.7799	8.4606
6.750%	12.3800	11.4824	10.7535	10.1510	9.6458	9.2169	8.8491	8.5308
6.875%	12.4431	11.5465	10.8187	10.2173	9.7131	9.2853	8.9185	8.6013

MONTHLY PAYMENT TO AMORTIZE A LOAN OF $1,000

Term of Loan

Interest Rate	17 Years	18 Years	19 Years	20 Years	21 Years	22 Years	23 Years	24 Years
2.000%	5.7865	5.5167	5.2756	5.0588	4.8630	4.6852	4.5232	4.3748
2.125%	5.8449	5.5754	5.3346	5.1182	4.9228	4.7453	4.5836	4.4356
2.250%	5.9036	5.6345	5.3941	5.1781	4.9830	4.8059	4.6445	4.4969
2.375%	5.9627	5.6940	5.4540	5.2383	5.0436	4.8669	4.7059	4.5587
2.500%	6.0222	5.7539	5.5143	5.2990	5.1047	4.9284	4.7678	4.6209
2.625%	6.0821	5.8142	5.5750	5.3601	5.1662	4.9904	4.8302	4.6837
2.750%	6.1423	5.8748	5.6360	5.4217	5.2282	5.0528	4.8930	4.7470
2.875%	6.2028	5.9358	5.6975	5.4836	5.2906	5.1156	4.9564	4.8108
3.000%	6.2637	5.9972	5.7594	5.5460	5.3534	5.1790	5.0202	4.8751
3.125%	6.3250	6.0590	5.8217	5.6088	5.4167	5.2427	5.0844	4.9399
3.250%	6.3867	6.1212	5.8844	5.6720	5.4804	5.3070	5.1492	5.0051
3.375%	6.4487	6.1837	5.9474	5.7356	5.5446	5.3717	5.2144	5.0709
3.500%	6.5110	6.2466	6.0109	5.7996	5.6092	5.4368	5.2801	5.1371
3.625%	6.5737	6.3099	6.0748	5.8640	5.6742	5.5024	5.3463	5.2039
3.750%	6.6368	6.3736	6.1390	5.9289	5.7396	5.5684	5.4129	5.2711
3.875%	6.7002	6.4376	6.2037	5.9941	5.8055	5.6349	5.4800	5.3387
4.000%	6.7639	6.5020	6.2687	6.0598	5.8718	5.7018	5.5475	5.4069
4.125%	6.8280	6.5667	6.3341	6.1259	5.9385	5.7692	5.6155	5.4755
4.250%	6.8925	6.6319	6.3999	6.1923	6.0056	5.8370	5.6840	5.5446
4.375%	6.9573	6.6974	6.4661	6.2592	6.0732	5.9052	5.7529	5.6142
4.500%	7.0225	6.7632	6.5327	6.3265	6.1412	5.9739	5.8222	5.6842
4.625%	7.0880	6.8295	6.5996	6.3942	6.2096	6.0430	5.8920	5.7547
4.750%	7.1538	6.8961	6.6670	6.4622	6.2784	6.1125	5.9623	5.8257
4.875%	7.2200	6.9630	6.7347	6.5307	6.3476	6.1824	6.0329	5.8971
5.000%	7.2866	7.0303	6.8028	6.5996	6.4172	6.2528	6.1041	5.9690
5.125%	7.3534	7.0980	6.8712	6.6688	6.4872	6.3236	6.1756	6.0413
5.250%	7.4206	7.1660	6.9401	6.7384	6.5576	6.3948	6.2476	6.1140
5.375%	7.4882	7.2344	7.0093	6.8085	6.6285	6.4664	6.3200	6.1872
5.500%	7.5561	7.3032	7.0789	6.8789	6.6997	6.5385	6.3929	6.2609
5.625%	7.6243	7.3723	7.1488	6.9497	6.7713	6.6109	6.4661	6.3350
5.750%	7.6929	7.4417	7.2191	7.0208	6.8434	6.6838	6.5398	6.4095
5.875%	7.7618	7.5115	7.2898	7.0924	6.9158	6.7571	6.6139	6.4844
6.000%	7.8310	7.5816	7.3608	7.1643	6.9886	6.8307	6.6885	6.5598
6.125%	7.9006	7.6521	7.4322	7.2366	7.0618	6.9048	6.7634	6.6356
6.250%	7.9705	7.7229	7.5040	7.3093	7.1353	6.9793	6.8387	6.7118
6.375%	8.0407	7.7941	7.5761	7.3823	7.2093	7.0541	6.9145	6.7884
6.500%	8.1112	7.8656	7.6486	7.4557	7.2836	7.1294	6.9906	6.8654
6.625%	8.1821	7.9375	7.7214	7.5295	7.3583	7.2050	7.0672	6.9429
6.750%	8.2533	8.0096	7.7945	7.6036	7.4334	7.2811	7.1441	7.0207
6.875%	8.3248	8.0822	7.8681	7.6781	7.5089	7.3575	7.2215	7.0990

MONTHLY PAYMENT TO AMORTIZE A LOAN OF $1,000

Term of Loan

Interest Rate	25 Years	26 Years	27 Years	28 Years	29 Years	30 Years	35 Years	40 Years
2.000%	4.2385	4.1130	3.9969	3.8893	3.7893	3.6962	3.3126	3.0283
2.125%	4.2997	4.1744	4.0587	3.9515	3.8518	3.7590	3.3771	3.0944
2.250%	4.3613	4.2364	4.1211	4.0142	3.9149	3.8225	3.4424	3.1614
2.375%	4.4235	4.2990	4.1840	4.0775	3.9786	3.8865	3.5083	3.2292
2.500%	4.4862	4.3621	4.2475	4.1414	4.0429	3.9512	3.5750	3.2978
2.625%	4.5494	4.4257	4.3115	4.2058	4.1078	4.0165	3.6423	3.3671
2.750%	4.6131	4.4899	4.3761	4.2709	4.1732	4.0824	3.7103	3.4373
2.875%	4.6774	4.5546	4.4413	4.3365	4.2393	4.1489	3.7791	3.5082
3.000%	4.7421	4.6198	4.5070	4.4027	4.3059	4.2160	3.8485	3.5798
3.125%	4.8074	4.6856	4.5733	4.4694	4.3732	4.2838	3.9186	3.6523
3.250%	4.8732	4.7519	4.6401	4.5367	4.4410	4.3521	3.9894	3.7254
3.375%	4.9394	4.8187	4.7074	4.6046	4.5094	4.4210	4.0608	3.7993
3.500%	5.0062	4.8860	4.7753	4.6730	4.5783	4.4904	4.1329	3.8739
3.625%	5.0735	4.9539	4.8437	4.7420	4.6478	4.5605	4.2057	3.9492
3.750%	5.1413	5.0222	4.9126	4.8115	4.7179	4.6312	4.2791	4.0253
3.875%	5.2096	5.0911	4.9821	4.8815	4.7885	4.7024	4.3531	4.1020
4.000%	5.2784	5.1605	5.0521	4.9521	4.8597	4.7742	4.4277	4.1794
4.125%	5.3476	5.2304	5.1226	5.0233	4.9315	4.8465	4.5030	4.2575
4.250%	5.4174	5.3008	5.1936	5.0949	5.0038	4.9194	4.5789	4.3362
4.375%	5.4876	5.3717	5.2652	5.1671	5.0766	4.9929	4.6555	4.4156
4.500%	5.5583	5.4430	5.3372	5.2398	5.1499	5.0669	4.7326	4.4956
4.625%	5.6295	5.5149	5.4098	5.3130	5.2238	5.1414	4.8103	4.5763
4.750%	5.7012	5.5873	5.4828	5.3868	5.2982	5.2165	4.8886	4.6576
4.875%	5.7733	5.6601	5.5564	5.4610	5.3732	5.2921	4.9674	4.7395
5.000%	5.8459	5.7334	5.6304	5.5357	5.4486	5.3682	5.0469	4.8220
5.125%	5.9190	5.8072	5.7049	5.6110	5.5246	5.4449	5.1269	4.9050
5.250%	5.9925	5.8815	5.7799	5.6867	5.6010	5.5220	5.2074	4.9887
5.375%	6.0665	5.9562	5.8554	5.7629	5.6780	5.5997	5.2885	5.0729
5.500%	6.1409	6.0314	5.9314	5.8397	5.7554	5.6779	5.3702	5.1577
5.625%	6.2157	6.1071	6.0078	5.9168	5.8334	5.7566	5.4523	5.2430
5.750%	6.2911	6.1832	6.0847	5.9945	5.9118	5.8357	5.5350	5.3289
5.875%	6.3668	6.2598	6.1620	6.0726	5.9907	5.9154	5.6182	5.4153
6.000%	6.4430	6.3368	6.2399	6.1512	6.0700	5.9955	5.7019	5.5021
6.125%	6.5196	6.4142	6.3181	6.2303	6.1499	6.0761	5.7861	5.5895
6.250%	6.5967	6.4921	6.3968	6.3098	6.2302	6.1572	5.8708	5.6774
6.375%	6.6742	6.5704	6.4760	6.3898	6.3109	6.2387	5.9559	5.7657
6.500%	6.7521	6.6492	6.5555	6.4702	6.3921	6.3207	6.0415	5.8546
6.625%	6.8304	6.7284	6.6356	6.5510	6.4738	6.4031	6.1276	5.9438
6.750%	6.9091	6.8079	6.7160	6.6323	6.5558	6.4860	6.2142	6.0336
6.875%	6.9883	6.8880	6.7969	6.7140	6.6384	6.5693	6.3011	6.1237

MONTHLY PAYMENT TO AMORTIZE A LOAN OF $1,000

Term of Loan

Interest Rate	1 Year	2 Years	3 Years	4 Years	5 Years	6 Years	7 Years	8 Years
7.000%	86.5267	44.7726	30.8771	23.9462	19.8012	17.0490	15.0927	13.6337
7.125%	86.5844	44.8293	30.9343	24.0043	19.8602	17.1091	15.1539	13.6960
7.250%	86.6420	44.8860	30.9915	24.0624	19.9194	17.1693	15.2152	13.7585
7.375%	86.6997	44.9428	31.0488	24.1206	19.9786	17.2296	15.2767	13.8211
7.500%	86.7574	44.9996	31.1062	24.1789	20.0379	17.2901	15.3383	13.8839
7.625%	86.8151	45.0565	31.1637	24.2373	20.0974	17.3507	15.4000	13.9468
7.750%	86.8729	45.1134	31.2212	24.2957	20.1570	17.4114	15.4620	14.0099
7.875%	86.9306	45.1703	31.2787	24.3543	20.2166	17.4723	15.5240	14.0732
8.000%	86.9884	45.2273	31.3364	24.4129	20.2764	17.5332	15.5862	14.1367
8.125%	87.0462	45.2843	31.3941	24.4716	20.3363	17.5943	15.6486	14.2003
8.250%	87.1041	45.3414	31.4518	24.5304	20.3963	17.6556	15.7111	14.2641
8.375%	87.1619	45.3985	31.5096	24.5893	20.4563	17.7169	15.7737	14.3280
8.500%	87.2198	45.4557	31.5675	24.6483	20.5165	17.7784	15.8365	14.3921
8.625%	87.2777	45.5129	31.6255	24.7074	20.5768	17.8400	15.8994	14.4564
8.750%	87.3356	45.5701	31.6835	24.7665	20.6372	17.9017	15.9625	14.5208
8.875%	87.3935	45.6274	31.7416	24.8257	20.6977	17.9636	16.0257	14.5854
9.000%	87.4515	45.6847	31.7997	24.8850	20.7584	18.0255	16.0891	14.6502
9.125%	87.5095	45.7421	31.8579	24.9444	20.8191	18.0876	16.1526	14.7151
9.250%	87.5675	45.7995	31.9162	25.0039	20.8799	18.1499	16.2162	14.7802
9.375%	87.6255	45.8570	31.9745	25.0635	20.9408	18.2122	16.2800	14.8455
9.500%	87.6835	45.9145	32.0329	25.1231	21.0019	18.2747	16.3440	14.9109
9.625%	87.7416	45.9720	32.0914	25.1829	21.0630	18.3373	16.4081	14.9765
9.750%	87.7997	46.0296	32.1499	25.2427	21.1242	18.4000	16.4723	15.0422
9.875%	87.8578	46.0873	32.2085	25.3026	21.1856	18.4629	16.5367	15.1081
10.000%	87.9159	46.1449	32.2672	25.3626	21.2470	18.5258	16.6012	15.1742
10.125%	87.9740	46.2026	32.3259	25.4227	21.3086	18.5889	16.6658	15.2404
10.250%	88.0322	46.2604	32.3847	25.4828	21.3703	18.6522	16.7306	15.3068
10.375%	88.0904	46.3182	32.4435	25.5431	21.4320	18.7155	16.7956	15.3733
10.500%	88.1486	46.3760	32.5024	25.6034	21.4939	18.7790	16.8607	15.4400
10.625%	88.2068	46.4339	32.5614	25.6638	21.5559	18.8426	16.9259	15.5069
10.750%	88.2651	46.4919	32.6205	25.7243	21.6180	18.9063	16.9913	15.5739
10.875%	88.3234	46.5498	32.6796	25.7849	21.6801	18.9701	17.0568	15.6411
11.000%	88.3817	46.6078	32.7387	25.8455	21.7424	19.0341	17.1224	15.7084
11.125%	88.4400	46.6659	32.7979	25.9063	21.8048	19.0982	17.1882	15.7759
11.250%	88.4983	46.7240	32.8572	25.9671	21.8673	19.1624	17.2542	15.8436
11.375%	88.5567	46.7821	32.9166	26.0280	21.9299	19.2267	17.3202	15.9114
11.500%	88.6151	46.8403	32.9760	26.0890	21.9926	19.2912	17.3865	15.9794
11.625%	88.6735	46.8985	33.0355	26.1501	22.0554	19.3557	17.4528	16.0475
11.750%	88.7319	46.9568	33.0950	26.2113	22.1183	19.4204	17.5193	16.1158
11.875%	88.7903	47.0151	33.1546	26.2725	22.1813	19.4853	17.5860	16.1842

MONTHLY PAYMENT TO AMORTIZE A LOAN OF $1,000

Term of Loan

Interest Rate	9 Years	10 Years	11 Years	12 Years	12 Years	14 Years	15 Years	16 Years
7.000%	12.5063	11.6108	10.8841	10.2838	9.7807	9.3540	8.9883	8.6721
7.125%	12.5697	11.6754	10.9497	10.3506	9.8486	9.4230	9.0583	8.7432
7.250%	12.6333	11.7401	11.0156	10.4176	9.9167	9.4922	9.1286	8.8146
7.375%	12.6971	11.8050	11.0817	10.4848	9.9851	9.5617	9.1992	8.8863
7.500%	12.7610	11.8702	11.1480	10.5523	10.0537	9.6314	9.2701	8.9583
7.625%	12.8252	11.9355	11.2145	10.6200	10.1226	9.7015	9.3413	9.0306
7.750%	12.8895	12.0011	11.2813	10.6879	10.1917	9.7718	9.4128	9.1032
7.875%	12.9540	12.0668	11.3483	10.7561	10.2611	9.8423	9.4845	9.1761
8.000%	13.0187	12.1328	11.4154	10.8245	10.3307	9.9132	9.5565	9.2493
8.125%	13.0836	12.1989	11.4829	10.8932	10.4006	9.9843	9.6288	9.3227
8.250%	13.1487	12.2653	11.5505	10.9621	10.4708	10.0557	9.7014	9.3965
8.375%	13.2139	12.3318	11.6183	11.0312	10.5412	10.1273	9.7743	9.4706
8.500%	13.2794	12.3986	11.6864	11.1006	10.6118	10.1992	9.8474	9.5449
8.625%	13.3450	12.4655	11.7547	11.1701	10.6827	10.2713	9.9208	9.6195
8.750%	13.4108	12.5327	11.8232	11.2400	10.7538	10.3438	9.9945	9.6945
8.875%	13.4767	12.6000	11.8919	11.3100	10.8252	10.4164	10.0684	9.7697
9.000%	13.5429	12.6676	11.9608	11.3803	10.8968	10.4894	10.1427	9.8452
9.125%	13.6093	12.7353	12.0299	11.4508	10.9687	10.5626	10.2172	9.9209
9.250%	13.6758	12.8033	12.0993	11.5216	11.0408	10.6360	10.2919	9.9970
9.375%	13.7425	12.8714	12.1689	11.5925	11.1131	10.7097	10.3670	10.0733
9.500%	13.8094	12.9398	12.2386	11.6637	11.1857	10.7837	10.4422	10.1499
9.625%	13.8764	13.0083	12.3086	11.7352	11.2586	10.8579	10.5178	10.2268
9.750%	13.9437	13.0770	12.3788	11.8068	11.3316	10.9324	10.5936	10.3039
9.875%	14.0111	13.1460	12.4493	11.8787	11.4049	11.0071	10.6697	10.3813
10.000%	14.0787	13.2151	12.5199	11.9508	11.4785	11.0820	10.7461	10.4590
10.125%	14.1465	13.2844	12.5907	12.0231	11.5523	11.1572	10.8227	10.5370
10.250%	14.2144	13.3539	12.6618	12.0957	11.6263	11.2327	10.8995	10.6152
10.375%	14.2826	13.4236	12.7330	12.1684	11.7005	11.3084	10.9766	10.6937
10.500%	14.3509	13.4935	12.8045	12.2414	11.7750	11.3843	11.0540	10.7724
10.625%	14.4193	13.5636	12.8761	12.3146	11.8497	11.4605	11.1316	10.8514
10.750%	14.4880	13.6339	12.9480	12.3880	11.9247	11.5370	11.2095	10.9307
10.875%	14.5568	13.7043	13.0201	12.4617	11.9999	11.6136	11.2876	11.0102
11.000%	14.6259	13.7750	13.0923	12.5356	12.0753	11.6905	11.3660	11.0900
11.125%	14.6950	13.8459	13.1648	12.6096	12.1509	11.7677	11.4446	11.1700
11.250%	14.7644	13.9169	13.2375	12.6839	12.2268	11.8451	11.5234	11.2503
11.375%	14.8339	13.9881	13.3104	12.7584	12.3029	11.9227	11.6026	11.3309
11.500%	14.9037	14.0595	13.3835	12.8332	12.3792	12.0006	11.6819	11.4116
11.625%	14.9735	14.1312	13.4568	12.9081	12.4557	12.0786	11.7615	11.4927
11.750%	15.0436	14.2029	13.5303	12.9833	12.5325	12.1570	11.8413	11.5740
11.875%	15.1138	14.2749	13.6040	13.0586	12.6095	12.2355	11.9214	11.6555

MONTHLY PAYMENT TO AMORTIZE A LOAN OF $1,000

Term of Loan

Interest Rate	17 Years	18 Years	19 Years	20 Years	21 Years	22 Years	23 Years	24 Years
7.000%	8.3966	8.1550	7.9419	7.7530	7.5847	7.4342	7.2992	7.1776
7.125%	8.4688	8.2282	8.0161	7.8282	7.6609	7.5114	7.3773	7.2566
7.250%	8.5412	8.3017	8.0907	7.9038	7.7375	7.5889	7.4558	7.3361
7.375%	8.6140	8.3756	8.1656	7.9797	7.8144	7.6668	7.5347	7.4159
7.500%	8.6871	8.4497	8.2408	8.0559	7.8917	7.7451	7.6139	7.4960
7.625%	8.7605	8.5242	8.3163	8.1325	7.9693	7.8237	7.6935	7.5766
7.750%	8.8342	8.5990	8.3922	8.2095	8.0473	7.9027	7.7735	7.6576
7.875%	8.9082	8.6742	8.4685	8.2868	8.1256	7.9821	7.8538	7.7389
8.000%	8.9826	8.7496	8.5450	8.3644	8.2043	8.0618	7.9345	7.8205
8.125%	9.0572	8.8254	8.6219	8.4424	8.2833	8.1418	8.0156	7.9026
8.250%	9.1321	8.9015	8.6991	8.5207	8.3627	8.2222	8.0970	7.9850
8.375%	9.2074	8.9779	8.7766	8.5993	8.4424	8.3030	8.1788	8.0677
8.500%	9.2829	9.0546	8.8545	8.6782	8.5224	8.3841	8.2609	8.1508
8.625%	9.3588	9.1316	8.9326	8.7575	8.6028	8.4655	8.3433	8.2343
8.750%	9.4349	9.2089	9.0111	8.8371	8.6834	8.5472	8.4261	8.3181
8.875%	9.5113	9.2865	9.0899	8.9170	8.7645	8.6293	8.5092	8.4022
9.000%	9.5880	9.3644	9.1690	8.9973	8.8458	8.7117	8.5927	8.4866
9.125%	9.6650	9.4427	9.2484	9.0778	8.9275	8.7945	8.6765	8.5714
9.250%	9.7423	9.5212	9.3281	9.1587	9.0094	8.8775	8.7606	8.6566
9.375%	9.8199	9.6000	9.4081	9.2398	9.0917	8.9609	8.8450	8.7420
9.500%	9.8978	9.6791	9.4884	9.3213	9.1743	9.0446	8.9297	8.8277
9.625%	9.9760	9.7585	9.5690	9.4031	9.2573	9.1286	9.0148	8.9138
9.750%	10.0544	9.8382	9.6499	9.4852	9.3405	9.2129	9.1002	9.0002
9.875%	10.1331	9.9182	9.7311	9.5675	9.4240	9.2975	9.1858	9.0869
10.000%	10.2121	9.9984	9.8126	9.6502	9.5078	9.3825	9.2718	9.1739
10.125%	10.2914	10.0790	9.8944	9.7332	9.5919	9.4677	9.3581	9.2612
10.250%	10.3709	10.1598	9.9764	9.8164	9.6763	9.5532	9.4447	9.3488
10.375%	10.4507	10.2409	10.0588	9.9000	9.7610	9.6390	9.5315	9.4366
10.500%	10.5308	10.3223	10.1414	9.9838	9.8460	9.7251	9.6187	9.5248
10.625%	10.6112	10.4039	10.2243	10.0679	9.9312	9.8114	9.7061	9.6133
10.750%	10.6918	10.4858	10.3075	10.1523	10.0168	9.8981	9.7938	9.7020
10.875%	10.7727	10.5680	10.3909	10.2370	10.1026	9.9850	9.8818	9.7910
11.000%	10.8538	10.6505	10.4746	10.3219	10.1887	10.0722	9.9701	9.8803
11.125%	10.9352	10.7332	10.5586	10.4071	10.2751	10.1597	10.0586	9.9698
11.250%	11.0169	10.8162	10.6429	10.4926	10.3617	10.2475	10.1474	10.0596
11.375%	11.0988	10.8994	10.7274	10.5783	10.4486	10.3355	10.2365	10.1497
11.500%	11.1810	10.9830	10.8122	10.6643	10.5358	10.4237	10.3258	10.2400
11.625%	11.2634	11.0667	10.8972	10.7506	10.6232	10.5123	10.4154	10.3306
11.750%	11.3461	11.1507	10.9825	10.8371	10.7109	10.6011	10.5052	10.4214
11.875%	11.4290	11.2350	11.0681	10.9238	10.7988	10.6901	10.5953	10.5125

MONTHLY PAYMENT TO AMORTIZE A LOAN OF $1,000

Term of Loan

Interest Rate	25 Years	26 Years	27 Years	28 Years	29 Years	30 Years	35 Years	40 Years
7.000%	7.0678	6.9684	6.8781	6.7961	6.7213	6.6530	6.3886	6.2143
7.125%	7.1477	7.0492	6.9598	6.8786	6.8047	6.7372	6.4764	6.3053
7.250%	7.2281	7.1304	7.0419	6.9616	6.8884	6.8218	6.5647	6.3967
7.375%	7.3088	7.2121	7.1244	7.0449	6.9726	6.9068	6.6533	6.4885
7.500%	7.3899	7.2941	7.2073	7.1287	7.0572	6.9921	6.7424	6.5807
7.625%	7.4714	7.3765	7.2906	7.2128	7.1422	7.0779	6.8319	6.6733
7.750%	7.5533	7.4593	7.3743	7.2974	7.2276	7.1641	6.9218	6.7662
7.875%	7.6355	7.5424	7.4584	7.3823	7.3133	7.2507	7.0120	6.8595
8.000%	7.7182	7.6260	7.5428	7.4676	7.3995	7.3376	7.1026	6.9531
8.125%	7.8012	7.7099	7.6276	7.5533	7.4860	7.4250	7.1936	7.0471
8.250%	7.8845	7.7942	7.7128	7.6393	7.5729	7.5127	7.2849	7.1414
8.375%	7.9682	7.8788	7.7983	7.7257	7.6601	7.6007	7.3766	7.2360
8.500%	8.0523	7.9638	7.8842	7.8125	7.7477	7.6891	7.4686	7.3309
8.625%	8.1367	8.0491	7.9705	7.8996	7.8357	7.7779	7.5610	7.4262
8.750%	8.2214	8.1348	8.0570	7.9871	7.9240	7.8670	7.6536	7.5217
8.875%	8.3065	8.2209	8.1440	8.0749	8.0126	7.9564	7.7466	7.6175
9.000%	8.3920	8.3072	8.2313	8.1630	8.1016	8.0462	7.8399	7.7136
9.125%	8.4777	8.3939	8.3189	8.2515	8.1909	8.1363	7.9335	7.8100
9.250%	8.5638	8.4810	8.4068	8.3403	8.2805	8.2268	8.0274	7.9066
9.375%	8.6502	8.5683	8.4950	8.4294	8.3705	8.3175	8.1216	8.0035
9.500%	8.7370	8.6560	8.5836	8.5188	8.4607	8.4085	8.2161	8.1006
9.625%	8.8240	8.7440	8.6725	8.6086	8.5513	8.4999	8.3109	8.1980
9.750%	8.9114	8.8323	8.7617	8.6986	8.6421	8.5915	8.4059	8.2956
9.875%	8.9990	8.9209	8.8512	8.7890	8.7333	8.6835	8.5012	8.3934
10.000%	9.0870	9.0098	8.9410	8.8796	8.8248	8.7757	8.5967	8.4915
10.125%	9.1753	9.0990	9.0311	8.9705	8.9165	8.8682	8.6925	8.5897
10.250%	9.2638	9.1885	9.1214	9.0618	9.0085	8.9610	8.7886	8.6882
10.375%	9.3527	9.2782	9.2121	9.1533	9.1008	9.0541	8.8848	8.7868
10.500%	9.4418	9.3683	9.3030	9.2450	9.1934	9.1474	8.9813	8.8857
10.625%	9.5312	9.4586	9.3943	9.3371	9.2862	9.2410	9.0781	8.9847
10.750%	9.6209	9.5492	9.4857	9.4294	9.3793	9.3348	9.1750	9.0840
10.875%	9.7109	9.6401	9.5775	9.5220	9.4727	9.4289	9.2722	9.1834
11.000%	9.8011	9.7313	9.6695	9.6148	9.5663	9.5232	9.3696	9.2829
11.125%	9.8916	9.8227	9.7618	9.7079	9.6601	9.6178	9.4672	9.3827
11.250%	9.9824	9.9143	9.8543	9.8012	9.7542	9.7126	9.5649	9.4826
11.375%	10.0734	10.0063	9.9471	9.8948	9.8486	9.8077	9.6629	9.5826
11.500%	10.1647	10.0984	10.0401	9.9886	9.9431	9.9029	9.7611	9.6828
11.625%	10.2562	10.1909	10.1333	10.0826	10.0379	9.9984	9.8594	9.7832
11.750%	10.3480	10.2835	10.2268	10.1769	10.1329	10.0941	9.9579	9.8836
11.875%	10.4400	10.3764	10.3205	10.2714	10.2281	10.1900	10.0566	9.9843

MONTHLY PAYMENT TO AMORTIZE A LOAN OF $1,000

Term of Loan

Interest Rate	1 Year	2 Years	3 Years	4 Years	5 Years	6 Years	7 Years	8 Years
12.000%	88.8488	47.0735	33.2143	26.3338	22.2444	19.5502	17.6527	16.2528
12.125%	88.9073	47.1319	33.2740	26.3953	22.3077	19.6153	17.7197	16.3216
12.250%	88.9658	47.1903	33.3338	26.4568	22.3710	19.6804	17.7867	16.3905
12.375%	89.0243	47.2488	33.3937	26.5183	22.4344	19.7457	17.8539	16.4596
12.500%	89.0829	47.3073	33.4536	26.5800	22.4979	19.8112	17.9212	16.5288
12.625%	89.1414	47.3659	33.5136	26.6417	22.5616	19.8767	17.9887	16.5982
12.750%	89.2000	47.4245	33.5737	26.7036	22.6253	19.9424	18.0563	16.6677
12.875%	89.2586	47.4831	33.6338	26.7655	22.6891	20.0082	18.1241	16.7374
13.000%	89.3173	47.5418	33.6940	26.8275	22.7531	20.0741	18.1920	16.8073
13.125%	89.3759	47.6006	33.7542	26.8896	22.8171	20.1401	18.2600	16.8773
13.250%	89.4346	47.6593	33.8145	26.9517	22.8813	20.2063	18.3282	16.9474
13.375%	89.4933	47.7182	33.8749	27.0140	22.9455	20.2726	18.3965	17.0177
13.500%	89.5520	47.7770	33.9353	27.0763	23.0098	20.3390	18.4649	17.0882
13.625%	89.6108	47.8359	33.9958	27.1387	23.0743	20.4055	18.5335	17.1588
13.750%	89.6695	47.8949	34.0563	27.2012	23.1388	20.4721	18.6022	17.2295
13.875%	89.7283	47.9539	34.1169	27.2638	23.2035	20.5389	18.6710	17.3004
14.000%	89.7871	48.0129	34.1776	27.3265	23.2683	20.6057	18.7400	17.3715
14.125%	89.8459	48.0720	34.2384	27.3892	23.3331	20.6727	18.8091	17.4427
14.250%	89.9048	48.1311	34.2992	27.4520	23.3981	20.7398	18.8784	17.5141
14.375%	89.9637	48.1902	34.3600	27.5150	23.4631	20.8071	18.9478	17.5856
14.500%	90.0225	48.2494	34.4210	27.5780	23.5283	20.8744	19.0173	17.6573
14.625%	90.0815	48.3087	34.4820	27.6410	23.5935	20.9419	19.0870	17.7291
14.750%	90.1404	48.3680	34.5430	27.7042	23.6589	21.0095	19.1568	17.8010
14.875%	90.1993	48.4273	34.6041	27.7674	23.7244	21.0772	19.2267	17.8731
15.000%	90.2583	48.4866	34.6653	27.8307	23.7899	21.1450	19.2968	17.9454
15.125%	90.3173	48.5461	34.7266	27.8942	23.8556	21.2130	19.3670	18.0178
15.250%	90.3763	48.6055	34.7879	27.9576	23.9214	21.2810	19.4373	18.0904
15.375%	90.4354	48.6650	34.8492	28.0212	23.9872	21.3492	19.5077	18.1631
15.500%	90.4944	48.7245	34.9107	28.0849	24.0532	21.4175	19.5783	18.2359
15.625%	90.5535	48.7841	34.9722	28.1486	24.1193	21.4859	19.6491	18.3089
15.750%	90.6126	48.8437	35.0337	28.2124	24.1854	21.5544	19.7199	18.3821
15.875%	90.6717	48.9034	35.0954	28.2763	24.2517	21.6231	19.7909	18.4554
16.000%	90.7309	48.9631	35.1570	28.3403	24.3181	21.6918	19.8621	18.5288
16.125%	90.7900	49.0229	35.2188	28.4043	24.3845	21.7607	19.9333	18.6024
16.250%	90.8492	49.0826	35.2806	28.4685	24.4511	21.8297	20.0047	18.6761
16.375%	90.9084	49.1425	35.3425	28.5327	24.5178	21.8988	20.0762	18.7500
16.500%	90.9676	49.2024	35.4044	28.5970	24.5845	21.9681	20.1479	18.8240
16.625%	91.0269	49.2623	35.4664	28.6614	24.6514	22.0374	20.2197	18.8981
16.750%	91.0862	49.3222	35.5284	28.7259	24.7184	22.1069	20.2916	18.9724
16.875%	91.1454	49.3822	35.5905	28.7904	24.7854	22.1764	20.3636	19.0469

MONTHLY PAYMENT TO AMORTIZE A LOAN OF $1,000

Term of Loan

Interest Rate	9 Years	10 Years	11 Years	12 Years	12 Years	14 Years	15 Years	16 Years
12.000%	15.1842	14.3471	13.6779	13.1342	12.6867	12.3143	12.0017	11.7373
12.125%	15.2548	14.4194	13.7520	13.2100	12.7641	12.3933	12.0822	11.8193
12.250%	15.3256	14.4920	13.8263	13.2860	12.8417	12.4725	12.1630	11.9015
12.375%	15.3965	14.5647	13.9007	13.3622	12.9196	12.5520	12.2440	11.9840
12.500%	15.4676	14.6376	13.9754	13.4386	12.9977	12.6317	12.3252	12.0667
12.625%	15.5388	14.7107	14.0503	13.5152	13.0760	12.7116	12.4067	12.1496
12.750%	15.6102	14.7840	14.1254	13.5920	13.1545	12.7917	12.4884	12.2328
12.875%	15.6818	14.8574	14.2006	13.6690	13.2332	12.8721	12.5703	12.3162
13.000%	15.7536	14.9311	14.2761	13.7463	13.3121	12.9526	12.6524	12.3999
13.125%	15.8255	15.0049	14.3518	13.8237	13.3912	13.0334	12.7348	12.4837
13.250%	15.8976	15.0789	14.4276	13.9013	13.4706	13.1144	12.8174	12.5678
13.375%	15.9699	15.1531	14.5036	13.9791	13.5502	13.1956	12.9002	12.6521
13.500%	16.0423	15.2274	14.5799	14.0572	13.6299	13.2771	12.9832	12.7367
13.625%	16.1149	15.3020	14.6563	14.1354	13.7099	13.3587	13.0664	12.8214
13.750%	16.1877	15.3767	14.7329	14.2138	13.7901	13.4406	13.1499	12.9064
13.875%	16.2606	15.4516	14.8097	14.2925	13.8704	13.5226	13.2335	12.9916
14.000%	16.3337	15.5266	14.8867	14.3713	13.9510	13.6049	13.3174	13.0770
14.125%	16.4070	15.6019	14.9638	14.4503	14.0318	13.6874	13.4015	13.1626
14.250%	16.4804	15.6773	15.0412	14.5295	14.1128	13.7701	13.4858	13.2484
14.375%	16.5540	15.7529	15.1187	14.6089	14.1940	13.8529	13.5703	13.3345
14.500%	16.6277	15.8287	15.1964	14.6885	14.2754	13.9360	13.6550	13.4207
14.625%	16.7016	15.9046	15.2743	14.7683	14.3570	14.0193	13.7399	13.5071
14.750%	16.7757	15.9807	15.3524	14.8483	14.4387	14.1028	13.8250	13.5938
14.875%	16.8499	16.0570	15.4307	14.9284	14.5207	14.1865	13.9104	13.6806
15.000%	16.9243	16.1335	15.5091	15.0088	14.6029	14.2704	13.9959	13.7677
15.125%	16.9989	16.2101	15.5878	15.0893	14.6852	14.3545	14.0816	13.8549
15.250%	17.0736	16.2869	15.6666	15.1700	14.7678	14.4388	14.1675	13.9424
15.375%	17.1485	16.3639	15.7456	15.2509	14.8505	14.5232	14.2536	14.0300
15.500%	17.2235	16.4411	15.8247	15.3320	14.9335	14.6079	14.3399	14.1179
15.625%	17.2987	16.5184	15.9041	15.4133	15.0166	14.6928	14.4264	14.2059
15.750%	17.3741	16.5958	15.9836	15.4948	15.0999	14.7778	14.5131	14.2941
15.875%	17.4496	16.6735	16.0633	15.5764	15.1834	14.8630	14.5999	14.3825
16.000%	17.5253	16.7513	16.1432	15.6583	15.2670	14.9485	14.6870	14.4711
16.125%	17.6011	16.8293	16.2232	15.7403	15.3509	15.0341	14.7743	14.5599
16.250%	17.6771	16.9074	16.3034	15.8224	15.4349	15.1199	14.8617	14.6488
16.375%	17.7532	16.9858	16.3838	15.9048	15.5192	15.2058	14.9493	14.7380
16.500%	17.8295	17.0642	16.4644	15.9873	15.6036	15.2920	15.0371	14.8273
16.625%	17.9059	17.1429	16.5451	16.0700	15.6881	15.3783	15.1251	14.9168
16.750%	17.9825	17.2217	16.6260	16.1529	15.7729	15.4648	15.2132	15.0065
16.875%	18.0593	17.3006	16.7071	16.2360	15.8578	15.5515	15.3015	15.0963

MONTHLY PAYMENT TO AMORTIZE A LOAN OF $1,000

Term of Loan

Interest Rate	17 Years	18 Years	19 Years	20 Years	21 Years	22 Years	23 Years	24 Years
12.000%	11.5122	11.3195	11.1539	11.0109	10.8870	10.7794	10.6856	10.6038
12.125%	11.5956	11.4043	11.2399	11.0981	10.9754	10.8689	10.7762	10.6954
12.250%	11.6792	11.4893	11.3262	11.1856	11.0641	10.9587	10.8670	10.7872
12.375%	11.7631	11.5745	11.4127	11.2734	11.1530	11.0487	10.9581	10.8792
12.500%	11.8473	11.6600	11.4995	11.3614	11.2422	11.1390	11.0494	10.9714
12.625%	11.9316	11.7457	11.5865	11.4496	11.3316	11.2294	11.1409	11.0639
12.750%	12.0162	11.8317	11.6738	11.5381	11.4212	11.3202	11.2326	11.1566
12.875%	12.1011	11.9179	11.7613	11.6268	11.5111	11.4111	11.3246	11.2495
13.000%	12.1861	12.0043	11.8490	11.7158	11.6011	11.5023	11.4168	11.3427
13.125%	12.2714	12.0910	11.9369	11.8049	11.6915	11.5937	11.5092	11.4360
13.250%	12.3570	12.1779	12.0251	11.8943	11.7820	11.6853	11.6018	11.5296
13.375%	12.4427	12.2650	12.1135	11.9839	11.8727	11.7771	11.6946	11.6233
13.500%	12.5287	12.3523	12.2021	12.0737	11.9637	11.8691	11.7876	11.7173
13.625%	12.6149	12.4399	12.2910	12.1638	12.0549	11.9613	11.8808	11.8114
13.750%	12.7013	12.5276	12.3800	12.2541	12.1463	12.0538	11.9743	11.9058
13.875%	12.7879	12.6156	12.4693	12.3445	12.2379	12.1464	12.0679	12.0003
14.000%	12.8748	12.7038	12.5588	12.4352	12.3297	12.2393	12.1617	12.0950
14.125%	12.9618	12.7922	12.6485	12.5261	12.4217	12.3323	12.2557	12.1900
14.250%	13.0491	12.8809	12.7384	12.6172	12.5139	12.4256	12.3500	12.2851
14.375%	13.1366	12.9697	12.8285	12.7085	12.6063	12.5190	12.4443	12.3803
14.500%	13.2242	13.0587	12.9188	12.8000	12.6989	12.6126	12.5389	12.4758
14.625%	13.3121	13.1480	13.0093	12.8917	12.7917	12.7065	12.6337	12.5714
14.750%	13.4002	13.2374	13.1000	12.9836	12.8847	12.8004	12.7286	12.6672
14.875%	13.4885	13.3271	13.1909	13.0756	12.9778	12.8946	12.8237	12.7632
15.000%	13.5770	13.4169	13.2820	13.1679	13.0712	12.9890	12.9190	12.8593
15.125%	13.6657	13.5069	13.3733	13.2603	13.1647	13.0835	13.0144	12.9556
15.250%	13.7546	13.5972	13.4647	13.3530	13.2584	13.1782	13.1100	13.0520
15.375%	13.8437	13.6876	13.5564	13.4458	13.3523	13.2731	13.2058	13.1486
15.500%	13.9329	13.7782	13.6483	13.5388	13.4464	13.3681	13.3018	13.2454
15.625%	14.0224	13.8690	13.7403	13.6320	13.5406	13.4633	13.3979	13.3423
15.750%	14.1120	13.9600	13.8325	13.7253	13.6350	13.5587	13.4941	13.4394
15.875%	14.2019	14.0511	13.9249	13.8189	13.7296	13.6542	13.5905	13.5366
16.000%	14.2919	14.1425	14.0175	13.9126	13.8243	13.7499	13.6871	13.6339
16.125%	14.3821	14.2340	14.1102	14.0064	13.9192	13.8457	13.7838	13.7314
16.250%	14.4725	14.3257	14.2031	14.1005	14.0143	13.9417	13.8806	13.8290
16.375%	14.5630	14.4176	14.2962	14.1946	14.1095	14.0379	13.9776	13.9268
16.500%	14.6538	14.5096	14.3894	14.2890	14.2048	14.1342	14.0747	14.0247
16.625%	14.7447	14.6018	14.4829	14.3835	14.3004	14.2306	14.1720	14.1227
16.750%	14.8358	14.6942	14.5764	14.4782	14.3960	14.3272	14.2694	14.2208
16.875%	14.9270	14.7868	14.6702	14.5730	14.4919	14.4239	14.3669	14.3191

MONTHLY PAYMENT TO AMORTIZE A LOAN OF $1,000

Term of Loan

Interest Rate	25 Years	26 Years	27 Years	28 Years	29 Years	30 Years	35 Years	40 Years
12.000%	10.5322	10.4695	10.4145	10.3661	10.3236	10.2861	10.1555	10.0850
12.125%	10.6247	10.5629	10.5087	10.4611	10.4192	10.3824	10.2545	10.1859
12.250%	10.7174	10.6565	10.6030	10.5562	10.5151	10.4790	10.3537	10.2869
12.375%	10.8104	10.7503	10.6977	10.6516	10.6112	10.5757	10.4531	10.3880
12.500%	10.9035	10.8443	10.7925	10.7471	10.7074	10.6726	10.5525	10.4892
12.625%	10.9969	10.9385	10.8875	10.8429	10.8039	10.7697	10.6522	10.5905
12.750%	11.0905	11.0329	10.9827	10.9388	10.9005	10.8669	10.7520	10.6920
12.875%	11.1843	11.1276	11.0781	11.0350	10.9973	10.9644	10.8519	10.7935
13.000%	11.2784	11.2224	11.1738	11.1313	11.0943	11.0620	10.9519	10.8951
13.125%	11.3726	11.3175	11.2696	11.2279	11.1915	11.1598	11.0521	10.9969
13.250%	11.4670	11.4127	11.3656	11.3246	11.2888	11.2577	11.1524	11.0987
13.375%	11.5616	11.5082	11.4618	11.4214	11.3864	11.3558	11.2529	11.2006
13.500%	11.6564	11.6038	11.5581	11.5185	11.4841	11.4541	11.3534	11.3026
13.625%	11.7515	11.6996	11.6547	11.6157	11.5819	11.5525	11.4541	11.4047
13.750%	11.8467	11.7956	11.7514	11.7131	11.6799	11.6511	11.5549	11.5069
13.875%	11.9420	11.8917	11.8483	11.8107	11.7781	11.7498	11.6557	11.6091
14.000%	12.0376	11.9881	11.9453	11.9084	11.8764	11.8487	11.7567	11.7114
14.125%	12.1334	12.0846	12.0425	12.0062	11.9749	11.9477	11.8578	11.8138
14.250%	12.2293	12.1813	12.1399	12.1043	12.0735	12.0469	11.9590	11.9162
14.375%	12.3254	12.2781	12.2375	12.2024	12.1722	12.1461	12.0603	12.0187
14.500%	12.4216	12.3751	12.3351	12.3007	12.2711	12.2456	12.1617	12.1213
14.625%	12.5181	12.4723	12.4330	12.3992	12.3701	12.3451	12.2632	12.2240
14.750%	12.6146	12.5696	12.5310	12.4978	12.4693	12.4448	12.3647	12.3267
14.875%	12.7114	12.6671	12.6291	12.5965	12.5686	12.5445	12.4664	12.4294
15.000%	12.8083	12.7647	12.7274	12.6954	12.6680	12.6444	12.5681	12.5322
15.125%	12.9054	12.8625	12.8258	12.7944	12.7675	12.7445	12.6699	12.6351
15.250%	13.0026	12.9604	12.9243	12.8935	12.8672	12.8446	12.7718	12.7380
15.375%	13.0999	13.0584	13.0230	12.9928	12.9669	12.9448	12.8738	12.8410
15.500%	13.1975	13.1566	13.1218	13.0922	13.0668	13.0452	12.9758	12.9440
15.625%	13.2951	13.2550	13.2208	13.1916	13.1668	13.1456	13.0780	13.0471
15.750%	13.3929	13.3534	13.3198	13.2913	13.2669	13.2462	13.1801	13.1502
15.875%	13.4908	13.4520	13.4190	13.3910	13.3671	13.3468	13.2824	13.2533
16.000%	13.5889	13.5507	13.5183	13.4908	13.4674	13.4476	13.3847	13.3565
16.125%	13.6871	13.6496	13.6178	13.5908	13.5679	13.5484	13.4871	13.4597
16.250%	13.7854	13.7485	13.7173	13.6908	13.6684	13.6493	13.5895	13.5630
16.375%	13.8839	13.8476	13.8169	13.7910	13.7690	13.7504	13.6920	13.6663
16.500%	13.9824	13.9468	13.9167	13.8912	13.8697	13.8515	13.7945	13.7696
16.625%	14.0811	14.0461	14.0166	13.9916	13.9705	13.9527	13.8971	13.8730
16.750%	14.1800	14.1456	14.1165	14.0921	14.0714	14.0540	13.9998	13.9764
16.875%	14.2789	14.2451	14.2166	14.1926	14.1724	14.1553	14.1025	14.0798

MONTHLY PAYMENT TO AMORTIZE A LOAN OF $1,000

Term of Loan

Interest Rate	1 Year	2 Years	3 Years	4 Years	5 Years	6 Years	7 Years	8 Years
17.000%	91.2048	49.4423	35.6527	28.8550	24.8526	22.2461	20.4358	19.1215
17.125%	91.2641	49.5023	35.7150	28.9198	24.9198	22.3159	20.5081	19.1962
17.250%	91.3234	49.5625	35.7773	28.9845	24.9872	22.3859	20.5805	19.2710
17.375%	91.3828	49.6226	35.8396	29.0494	25.0547	22.4559	20.6531	19.3461
17.500%	91.4422	49.6828	35.9021	29.1144	25.1222	22.5260	20.7258	19.4212
17.625%	91.5016	49.7431	35.9646	29.1794	25.1899	22.5963	20.7986	19.4965
17.750%	91.5611	49.8034	36.0271	29.2445	25.2576	22.6667	20.8716	19.5719
17.875%	91.6205	49.8637	36.0897	29.3097	25.3255	22.7372	20.9446	19.6475
18.000%	91.6800	49.9241	36.1524	29.3750	25.3934	22.8078	21.0178	19.7232
18.125%	91.7395	49.9845	36.2151	29.4404	25.4615	22.8785	21.0912	19.7991
18.250%	91.7990	50.0450	36.2779	29.5058	25.5296	22.9493	21.1646	19.8751
18.375%	91.8586	50.1055	36.3408	29.5713	25.5979	23.0203	21.2382	19.9512
18.500%	91.9181	50.1660	36.4037	29.6369	25.6662	23.0914	21.3119	20.0274
18.625%	91.9777	50.2266	36.4667	29.7026	25.7346	23.1625	21.3858	20.1038
18.750%	92.0373	50.2872	36.5297	29.7684	25.8032	23.2338	21.4597	20.1804
18.875%	92.0969	50.3479	36.5929	29.8342	25.8718	23.3052	21.5338	20.2571
19.000%	92.1566	50.4086	36.6560	29.9001	25.9406	23.3767	21.6080	20.3339

MONTHLY PAYMENT TO AMORTIZE A LOAN OF $1,000

Term of Loan

Interest Rate	9 Years	10 Years	11 Years	12 Years	12 Years	14 Years	15 Years	16 Years
17.000%	18.1362	17.3798	16.7883	16.3192	15.9430	15.6384	15.3900	15.1863
17.125%	18.2132	17.4591	16.8697	16.4026	16.0282	15.7254	15.4787	15.2765
17.250%	18.2905	17.5385	16.9513	16.4862	16.1137	15.8126	15.5676	15.3669
17.375%	18.3678	17.6181	17.0330	16.5700	16.1993	15.9000	15.6566	15.4574
17.500%	18.4453	17.6979	17.1149	16.6539	16.2851	15.9876	15.7458	15.5481
17.625%	18.5230	17.7778	17.1970	16.7380	16.3711	16.0753	15.8351	15.6390
17.750%	18.6008	17.8579	17.2792	16.8222	16.4572	16.1632	15.9247	15.7300
17.875%	18.6788	17.9381	17.3616	16.9066	16.5435	16.2513	16.0144	15.8212
18.000%	18.7569	18.0185	17.4442	16.9912	16.6300	16.3395	16.1042	15.9126
18.125%	18.8351	18.0991	17.5269	17.0759	16.7166	16.4279	16.1942	16.0041
18.250%	18.9136	18.1798	17.6098	17.1608	16.8034	16.5165	16.2844	16.0957
18.375%	18.9921	18.2606	17.6928	17.2459	16.8904	16.6052	16.3747	16.1875
18.500%	19.0708	18.3417	17.7760	17.3311	16.9775	16.6941	16.4652	16.2795
18.625%	19.1497	18.4228	17.8593	17.4165	17.0648	16.7831	16.5559	16.3716
18.750%	19.2287	18.5041	17.9428	17.5021	17.1523	16.8723	16.6467	16.4639
18.875%	19.3078	18.5856	18.0265	17.5878	17.2399	16.9616	16.7376	16.5564
19.000%	19.3871	18.6672	18.1103	17.6736	17.3276	17.0511	16.8288	16.6489

MONTHLY PAYMENT TO AMORTIZE A LOAN OF $1,000

Term of Loan

Interest Rate	17 Years	18 Years	19 Years	20 Years	21 Years	22 Years	23 Years	24 Years
17.000%	15.0184	14.8795	14.7641	14.6680	14.5878	14.5208	14.4646	14.4175
17.125%	15.1100	14.9724	14.8581	14.7631	14.6839	14.6178	14.5624	14.5160
17.250%	15.2018	15.0654	14.9524	14.8584	14.7802	14.7149	14.6603	14.6147
17.375%	15.2937	15.1586	15.0467	14.9538	14.8766	14.8122	14.7584	14.7134
17.500%	15.3858	15.2519	15.1412	15.0494	14.9731	14.9095	14.8565	14.8123
17.625%	15.4780	15.3455	15.2359	15.1451	15.0698	15.0071	14.9548	14.9113
17.750%	15.5704	15.4391	15.3307	15.2410	15.1666	15.1047	15.0532	15.0104
17.875%	15.6630	15.5329	15.4257	15.3370	15.2635	15.2025	15.1518	15.1096
18.000%	15.7557	15.6269	15.5208	15.4331	15.3605	15.3004	15.2504	15.2089
18.125%	15.8486	15.7210	15.6160	15.5294	15.4577	15.3984	15.3492	15.3083
18.250%	15.9416	15.8153	15.7114	15.6258	15.5550	15.4965	15.4480	15.4078
18.375%	16.0348	15.9097	15.8069	15.7223	15.6525	15.5948	15.5470	15.5074
18.500%	16.1281	16.0042	15.9026	15.8190	15.7500	15.6931	15.6461	15.6071
18.625%	16.2216	16.0989	15.9984	15.9158	15.8477	15.7916	15.7452	15.7069
18.750%	16.3152	16.1938	16.0943	16.0127	15.9455	15.8902	15.8445	15.8068
18.875%	16.4090	16.2887	16.1904	16.1097	16.0434	15.9889	15.9439	15.9068
19.000%	16.5029	16.3838	16.2866	16.2068	16.1414	16.0876	16.0434	16.0069

MONTHLY PAYMENT TO AMORTIZE A LOAN OF $1,000

Term of Loan

Interest Rate	25 Years	26 Years	27 Years	28 Years	29 Years	30 Years	35 Years	40 Years
17.000%	14.3780	14.3447	14.3168	14.2933	14.2734	14.2568	14.2053	14.1832
17.125%	14.4771	14.4445	14.4171	14.3940	14.3746	14.3583	14.3081	14.2867
17.250%	14.5764	14.5443	14.5174	14.4948	14.4758	14.4599	14.4109	14.3902
17.375%	14.6758	14.6443	14.6179	14.5957	14.5771	14.5615	14.5138	14.4938
17.500%	14.7753	14.7443	14.7184	14.6967	14.6785	14.6633	14.6168	14.5973
17.625%	14.8749	14.8445	14.8191	14.7978	14.7800	14.7651	14.7197	14.7009
17.750%	14.9746	14.9447	14.9198	14.8989	14.8815	14.8669	14.8228	14.8045
17.875%	15.0744	15.0451	15.0206	15.0002	14.9831	14.9689	14.9258	14.9082
18.000%	15.1743	15.1455	15.1215	15.1015	15.0848	15.0709	15.0289	15.0118
18.125%	15.2743	15.2460	15.2225	15.2029	15.1865	15.1729	15.1321	15.1155
18.250%	15.3744	15.3466	15.3235	15.3043	15.2883	15.2750	15.2352	15.2192
18.375%	15.4746	15.4473	15.4247	15.4059	15.3902	15.3772	15.3384	15.3229
18.500%	15.5748	15.5481	15.5259	15.5075	15.4922	15.4794	15.4417	15.4266
18.625%	15.6752	15.6489	15.6272	15.6091	15.5942	15.5817	15.5449	15.5304
18.750%	15.7757	15.7499	15.7285	15.7109	15.6962	15.6841	15.6483	15.6342
18.875%	15.8762	15.8509	15.8300	15.8127	15.7983	15.7865	15.7516	15.7379
19.000%	15.9768	15.9520	15.9315	15.9145	15.9005	15.8889	15.8549	15.8417

GLOSSARY

addendum: An addition to a contract.

adjustable-rate mortgage (ARM): A loan with an interest rate that is periodically adjusted by the lender.

agreement of sale: A document the buyer initiates and the seller approves that details the price and terms of a proposed transaction. Not used in every state.

amenities: Special features in a home or housing development. Central air-conditioning, pools, hot tubs, and modern built-in appliances are good examples of amenities.

American Society of Home Inspectors (ASHI): A professional association of independent home inspectors whose members must meet the group's education and performance requirements. You can call 800-743-2744 for a list of ASHI certified inspectors in your area, or visit its Web site at http://www.ashi.com.

amortization: The process of paying the principal and interest on a loan through installments.

amortize: To pay off a loan in (typically monthly) installments.

application: A document that details a potential borrower's income, debt, and other obligations to determine creditworthiness.

application fee: The fee that a lender charges to process a loan application.

appraisal: An opinion of the value of a property at a given point in time.

appraisal fee: The fee that an appraiser charges to estimate the market value of a home or other property.

appreciation: An increase in the value of a home or other property.

asking price: The price a seller sets or "asks" for a home.

back-end ratio: The ratio, or percentage, that a lender uses to compare a borrower's total debt (principal, interest, property taxes, and insurance plus other monthly debt payments) to gross monthly income. [See: front-end ratio.]

backup offer: A secondary bid for a property that a seller agrees to accept if the first offer from a different buyer fails.

balloon loan: A mortgage in which monthly installments are not large enough to repay the loan by the end of the term. As a result, the final payment due is the lump sum of the remaining principal.

balloon payment: The final lump sum payment due at the end of a balloon loan. Unless the borrower has a lot of cash, the home must usually be sold or the loan refinanced to pay the big lump sum.

bonus room: A room with no specifically designated function, unlike a bedroom or dining room. Many owners and buyers use a bonus room as a library, home office, sewing room, or nursery.

broker: A broker is anyone who acts as a go-between. A real estate broker is licensed to represent buyers and sellers in real estate transactions. A mortgage broker is an individual or firm that helps borrowers find mortgage loans.

built-ins: Appliances or other items that are framed into a home or permanently attached to its walls. Built-ins can't easily be removed, which is why the items are usually included in the sale of a home.

burrow: A burrow is a hole in the ground. A burro is a donkey-like animal. Now that you've read this book, we hope you know the difference.

The Buyer's Agent, Inc.: A national buyer's brokerage company with franchises in about 40 states. Call 800-766-8728 for information and referrals or visit its Web site (http://www.forbuyers.com).

buyer's market: A slow real estate market in which buyers have an advantage over sellers.

bylaws: The rules and regulations that a homeowners association or corporation adopts to govern activities.

cancellation clause: A clause in a contract that details the conditions under which either the buyer or seller can terminate the agreement.

cap: A limit on the amount that the interest rate or monthly payment can increase in an adjustable-rate mortgage. Most ARMs have two caps: One prevents the rate or payment from rising above a preset level at each adjustment period, while the other prevents the rate or monthly payment from climbing above a specified limit over the life of the loan.

carport: A roof that covers a driveway or other parking area.

certificate of eligibility: A document issued by the Veterans Administration that verifies the eligibility of a veteran of the armed forces to take part in the VA's special mortgage programs.

chattel: Personal property, typically including furniture, pictures that hang on a wall, and freestanding appliances that can easily be moved. Chattel property is usually not included in the sales price of a home, so sellers can usually take the items when they move out.

closing: The final procedure in a home sale, when the last documents are signed and recorded and title to the property is transferred from the seller to the buyer.

closing costs: Transaction-related expenses, such as loan fees and appraisal charges.

comparables: Properties used as comparisons to determine the value of a certain home. Typically referred to as "comps."

condominium: An individual unit in a building or development. The homeowner holds title to the interior space and shares ownership of common areas (such as parking lots or a pool) with other owners in the building or development.

conforming loan: A mortgage that meets the qualifications to be purchased by the Federal National Mortgage Association (Fannie Mae) or Federal Home Loan Mortgage Corporation (Freddie Mac). Rates on conforming loans are often lower than rates on nonconforming loans.

contingency: A condition specified in a purchase contract. If the contingency is not met, the sale can usually be canceled and the buyer can have the deposit returned.

credit report: A report from a credit bureau that shows a loan applicant's history of payments made on previous debts.

deed of trust: A document that gives a lender the right to foreclose on a property if the borrower defaults on the loan.

deposit: Money given by the buyer with an offer to purchase property. Also called *earnest money.*

dry rot: A fungal decay that causes wood to become brittle and crumble.

earnest money: Money a buyer gives with an offer to purchase a property. Also called a *deposit.*

Equal Credit Opportunity Act (ECOA): The federal law that prohibits a lender or other creditor from refusing to grant credit based on an applicant's sex, marital status, race, religion, national origin, or age, or because the applicant receives public assistance.

escrow agent: A neutral third party who ensures that all conditions of a real estate transaction are met. Not used in all states.

Fannie Mae: Nickname of the Federal National Mortgage Association, a publicly held company that buys mortgages from lenders and resells them as securities on the secondary mortgage market. The process ensures that lenders always have enough cash to make new loans.

Federal Housing Administration (FHA): A government agency that operates a variety of home loan programs, some of which can be used by buyers with down payments as small as 3 percent or 5 percent.

first mortgage: The primary mortgage on a property that has priority over all other mortgages.

fixed-rate mortgage: A home loan with an interest rate that will remain at a specific rate for the term of the loan.

for sale by owner (FSBO): A property offered by a seller who has not hired a professional sales agent. Pronounced "fizz-bo."

Freddie Mac: Nickname of Federal Home Loan Mortgage Corporation, which buys mortgages from lenders and resells them as securities on the secondary mortgage market. The process ensures that lenders always have enough cash to make new loans.

front-end ratio: The ratio, or percentage, that a lender uses to compare a borrower's monthly housing expense (principal, interest, property taxes, and insurance) to gross monthly income. [See: back-end ratio.]

good faith estimate: An estimate that a lender must provide to a prospective borrower that shows the costs the borrower will incur for loan processing charges, fees, and the like.

gross income: A borrower's total income before taxes or expenses are subtracted.

half-bath: A bathroom with a toilet and sink but no tub or shower. Sometimes called a *powder room*.

hazard insurance: An insurance policy that protects against damage caused by fire, wind, and many other dangers. Buyers must usually purchase the insurance before a lender will issue a loan.

homeowners association: A group that sets and enforces rules in a condominium or town house development or a planned community of single-family homes.

home warranty: A type of insurance that covers repairs to certain parts of a house and some fixtures after a buyer moves in.

impounds: The portion of a monthly mortgage payment that the lender places in a special account to pay for hazard insurance, property taxes, or other bills as they become due. Not all lenders require borrowers to have an impound account.

inspection report: A report, usually prepared by a professional inspector, that summarizes the condition of a home's various components.

joint tenancy: An ownership arrangement by two or more people that gives each person an interest in a home. When one owner dies, the interest in the property usually passes to the other owner(s).

jumbo loan: A loan that exceeds the limits set by Fannie Mae and Freddie Mac.

late charge: A fee a lender imposes on a borrower when payment on the mortgage was not received by its due date.

loan-to-value ratio (LTV): A technical measure lenders use to assess the relationship of the loan amount to the value of the property. A borrower seeking an $85,000 loan to purchase a home valued at $100,000 would have an LTV of 85 percent.

low-documentation loan: A mortgage that requires only minimal verification of the borrower's income and assets. Most "low-doc" loans require a down payment of at least 20 percent or 25 percent.

margin: A lender's retail markup on an adjustable-rate mortgage. If an ARM's index rate is 5 percent and the lender charges a 2.5 percentage point margin, the borrower's actual loan rate will be 7.5 percent.

mortgage: A legal document specifying a certain amount of money to purchase a home at a certain interest rate and using the property as collateral. Similar to a trust deed.

mortgage banker: A company that provides home loans using its own money. Typically, the company then sells the loans to investors.

mortgage broker: A person or company who helps borrowers find a lender. The broker doesn't make the loan but receives payment from the lender for services.

mortgage life insurance: A special type of insurance that will pay off a mortgage if the borrower dies before the debt is retired. Usually a waste of money, because most borrowers can obtain a traditional life insurance policy for the same amount of coverage at far less cost.

move-up buyer: A person who sells a house in order to purchase another home that's larger or in a nicer neighborhood.

negative amortization: A nasty proposition in which the borrower's scheduled monthly payment is too small to cover both the principal and interest on the loan, which means the outstanding balance of the loan will actually grow larger with each payment. Many adjustable-rate mortgages are susceptible to "neg-am," but smart borrowers never take them.

note: The legal document that requires a borrower to repay a mortgage at a certain interest rate over a specified period of time.

note rate: The interest rate specified in a mortgage note.

online listing: A home or other property that's advertised over the Internet.

open house: A marketing event, held by a seller or real estate agent, in which prospective buyers can walk through the home to determine if they'd like to buy it.

patent defect: An easily detectable deficiency in a property, such as a sagging floor, leaking roof, or uneven yard.

PITI: Lender jargon for a borrower's monthly payment for principal and interest on a proposed loan, combined with the taxes and insurance needed to maintain the property.

points: Fees a lender charges to a borrower when a loan is issued. One point is equal to 1 percent of the loan amount.

portfolio lender: A lender who makes loans with its own money and then keeps the loans on the company's books—in other words, inside its "portfolio"—rather than selling the loans to outside investors.

prepayment penalty: A charge lenders can levy on borrowers who pay their loan off early, whether the home is sold or the property is refinanced. Most fixed-rate mortgages include prepayment penalties, but many adjustable-rate mortgages do not.

private mortgage insurance (PMI): A special type of loan insurance that many lenders require borrowers to purchase if the borrower's down payment is less than 20 percent of the home's purchase price. If the borrower defaults, the insurer will reimburse the lender for its losses.

purchase offer: A written offer, made by a buyer, to purchase a property from a seller.

real estate agent: A person licensed to represent buyers or sellers in real estate transactions for a fee or commission. Unless they also have a broker's license, agents must work directly for a real estate broker or brokerage company.

real estate broker: A person or corporation licensed to represent buyers or sellers for a fee or commission. Brokers may also supervise transactions involving other real estate agents.

real property: Land and any permanent fixtures on it, including homes, other structures, fences, and trees.

REALTOR©: A professional designation for an agent or broker who belongs to the National Association of REALTORS© and promises to abide by the association's Code of Ethics. About half of all licensees, including most full-timers, are members of NAR.

recorder: The local official or public agency responsible for keeping real estate records, such as the legal owner of each home.

recording: The act of filing a document, such as a trust deed, with the local recorder.

sales contract: A contract that details the terms of a transaction. It must be signed by both the buyer and the seller to be valid.

seller carryback: An agreement in which the seller provides financing for a home purchase. Also known as a *takeback*.

seller takeback: See above.

slab foundation: A foundation built directly on soil, with no crawl space or basement.

survey: A precise measurement of a property taken by a licensed surveyor.

teaser rate: An unusually low, short-term rate offered by a lender to a borrower. The rate will increase when the teaser period ends.

tenancy by the entirety: A method of holding title to a property by a husband and wife. When one spouse dies, his or her interest passes to the other spouse. Not available in all states.

tenancy in common: A method of holding title in which two or more owners hold an undivided (but not necessarily equal) interest in a property, with no automatic right of survivorship.

title: The legal document that confers ownership of a home or other real property.

title company: A company that ensures that a seller has the clear legal right to sell a property and then issues a title insurance policy to protect the buyer or lender against possible challenges to the buyer's new title.

title insurance: A policy issued to lenders or buyers to protect against losses caused by an unexpected dispute over ownership of a property.

title search: A check of public title records to ascertain that the seller is the legal owner and that there are no unknown claims or liens against the property.

town house: An attached home that is not a condominium.

tract home: A mass-produced home in a development built by one builder. Sometimes called a *production home*.

transfer tax: An assessment made by state or local authorities when property is transferred from one owner to another.

Truth-in-Lending Act: The federal law that allows a consumer to cancel a home-improvement loan, second mortgage, or certain other types of loans until midnight of the third business day after a contract is signed, provided that the contract calls for the home to be pledged as collateral.

unsecured loan: Any loan that is not backed by collateral.

VA loans: Loans guaranteed by the Veterans Administration that allow veterans of the armed forces to purchase a home or other property with little or no down payment.

verification of deposit: A document used in the loan process in which the lender asks the loan applicant's primary bank to verify the borrower's account balances and history.

verification of employment: A document used in the loan process in which the lender asks the loan applicant's employer to confirm the borrower's position and salary.

Veterans Administration (VA): The U.S. Department of Veterans Affairs. It operates a variety of mortgage programs that allow veterans of the armed forces to purchase a home or other property with little or no down payment.

walk-through: A buyer's final inspection of the home to determine if all conditions in the original purchase agreement have been satisfied. The walk-through is typically conducted between 24 and 72 hours before the final closing documents are signed.

zoning: Government regulations that control how property is used within its jurisdiction. For example, most cities have zoning ordinances that prohibit businesses from opening a store or shop in an area that is meant for residential use only.

zoning variance: A waiver granted by local officials to a local zoning ordinance. For example, a freelance graphic artist might ask for a variance from an ordinance that bans businesses from operating in residential areas so the artist could work from home.

RESOURCES

Books

The Common-Sense Mortgage. Peter G. Miller (NTC/Contemporary Books). One of the best and most comprehensive guides to your various mortgage options, with special emphasis on issues that affect first-time buyers.

The Homebuyer's Kit: Finding Your Dream Home, Financing Your Purchase, Making the Best Deal, Gaining Tax Benefits. Edith Lank. (Dearborn). Written years ago but updated frequently, it's still one of the best step-by-step guides for buyers that has ever been published.

The Homebuying Game: A Quick and Easy Way to Get the Best Home for Your Money. Julie Garton-Good. (Dearborn). Another comprehensive guide for buyers, loaded with "inside tips" to help you get the best deal on a house and loan.

Newsletters

The three newsletters below provide money-saving tips on a variety of topics that interest homebuyers and homeowners, from finding the best mortgage deal to slashing your expenses after you move in. Each charges an annual subscription fee but they'll provide you with a free copy of their most current newsletter if you send them a self-addressed, stamped envelope and mention this book in your request.

Cheapskate Monthly, P.O. Box 2135, Paramount, CA 90723

The Penny Pincher, P.O. Box 809, Kings Park, NY 11754

The Tightwad Gazette, R.R. 1, Box 3570, Leeds, ME 04263

Online Resources

There are now more than 50,000 real-estate-related Web sites on the Internet, with literally dozens being added every day. It's impossible to view them all but the ones below have consistently remained among the best.

Our Top Five Favorites

homeadvisor.com: Launched in 1998 by Microsoft Corp., it's an online step-by-step guide that leads you through the homebuying process. Features about one million property listings, a detailed glossary, lots of helpful calculators, and a nifty tool to help you find the best mortgage. In the interest of full disclosure, the author of this book provided much of the site's editorial content.

homeshark.com: Another comprehensive real estate site, chockful of listings and consumer information. Also has links to other good sites, especially those that provide information about a community's demographics and schools.

ired.com: One of the oldest and biggest real estate sites on the Internet, operated by the aptly named International Read Estate Directory. Includes a terrific search engine to help you find online information about virtually every real estate topic possible.

money.com: The official site of *Money* magazine, it's got lots of useful information about buying a home and getting a loan, plus plenty of links to related sites recommended by the magazine's editors.

realtor.com: The official site of the National Association of Realtors, it's got more online property listings than any other Web site and a feature to help you find an agent in your area. Also includes a directory of child care and elder care centers, plus a neat tool to help you change your address online.

Other Great Internet Web Sites

amshomefinder.com: An excellent source of information about the demographics and schools in thousands of communities across the U.S.

ashi.com: Operated by the American Society of Home Inspectors, the largest trade association for professional inspectors. Provides a referral system, plus useful information concerning inspection related issues.

bankrate.com: Operated by the respected Bank Rate Monitor newsletter, includes daily updates on mortgage rates and lots of good tips for loan seekers.

cyberhomes.com: Offers more than one million online property listings. Also offers free school reports, calculators, and other financial tools.

dataquick.com: Can provide up to 30 comparable home sales for an area you select but charges a fee for the service.

e-loan.com: An Internet mortgage broker, it's got some useful calculators and an e-mail "alert system" that tells you when rates move up or down.

equifax.com: Operated by credit reporting giant Equifax, it features basic information about credit and allows you to order a report online.

experian.com: Our favorite site for credit-related information. Lets you order a credit report online, includes a biweekly question-and-answer column, and contains lots of general information about credit. Also provides recent sales data for about 30 states for a fee.

hsh.com: One of the most comprehensive online sources of mortgage rate information, updated several times a day. Includes a good library for consumers and a special area for borrowers who've had some recent credit problems.

improvenet.com: Provides referrals to contractors, architects, product suppliers, and a handful of lenders who've passed the operator's basic financial and legal tests.

inman.com: A free site operated by Inman Group, a respected online news agency. Features about 20 new real estate stories a day, plus links to useful sites that include the consumer oriented "Real Estate Center" operated by nationally syndicated real estate columnist Robert J. Bruss.

interest.com: Another good loan related site with financial calculators, current mortgage rates, and a library of stories designed to help buyers seeking a loan and homeowners planning to refinance.

kingfeatures.com: Features the weekly "About Real Estate" column that's published in about 100 newspapers across the nation by David W. Myers, who also wrote this book. Click on the "features" button and then click the "About Real Estate" heading.

newhomesearch.com: Perhaps the largest listing service for builders of new homes. Includes a nice feature that lets you search for newly built homes in your price range and, in some cases, view actual floor plans.

ourbroker.com: One of the Internet's most comprehensive real estate sites, it's operated by real estate author Peter G. Miller. It includes a good glossary, loads of consumer-oriented information, and a thorough question-and-answer database.

owners.com: A site that specializes in listing properties that are offered directly by the seller, rather than through a real estate agent.

quickenmortgage.com: Another Internet mortgage broker, nice features include a credit report analyzer and several good calculators—including perhaps the best online calculator to help you determine how much money you can borrow.

transunion.com: Operated by credit reporting giant Trans Union Corp., it has basic credit information and allows you to order a report online for a nominal fee.

INDEX